ROMAN
WARFARE

ROMAN WARFARE

ADRIAN GOLDSWORTHY

General Editor: John Keegan

CASSELL&CO

Cassell, Wellington House, 125 Strand, London WC2R 0BB

First published in Great Britain, 2000
This paperback edition 2002

British Library Cataloguing-in-publication Data
ISBN: 0-304-36265-4

Cartography: Arcadia Editions Ltd
Designer: Richard Carr
Picture research: Elaine Willis
Printed and bound in Spain

Title Page: *Praetorian guardsmen in parade uniforms from the Arch of Claudius.*
Overleaf: *The Arch of Constantine was erected in Rome in* AD 315, *but made use of
many sculptures from earlier monuments. These scenes show Marcus Aurelius
making a speech to a parade of soldiers.*

Acknowledgements

THIS BOOK HAS been a pleasure to write and I should like to thank all the friends and family who read and commented on the various drafts, notably Ian Haynes, Julian Deeks and especially Ian Hughes. The latter took part, along with Glyn Quigley, in a highly stimulating series of seminars on the Second Punic War run jointly by Louis Rawlings and myself as part of the Cardiff University MA programme in 1996–7. Several of the ideas in the second chapter were derived from the discussions in these sessions. I have followed Louis' ideas on early Roman warfare extensively in the first chapter. Similarly, in chapter 5, I have drawn much inspiration from Hugh Elton's splendid *Warfare in Roman Europe* and it is appropriate for me to acknowledge my debt to both of them. However, the views expressed here are my own and not necessarily shared by either scholar. I would also like to express my thanks to the team at Cassell, and especially Penny Gardiner, for all their work on the volume, and to Malcolm Swanston for his splendid maps and illustrations.

Adrian Goldsworthy
Penarth

Contents

KEY TO MAPS

Political colours

▭	Roman Empire
▨	dependent state unless otherwise indicated

Symbols on map

✕	battle
⌂	fort
✸	siege

Name style

PARTHIAN EMPIRE	independent state
Thrace	province
SARMATIANS	major tribal group

Geographical symbols

◪	urban area
——	Roman road
——	river
- - -	seasonal river
······	canal
▬▬	border

Military movements

➤	attack
-➤	retreat

Map list

Chronology

This chart lists the major military events in Rome's history that can be securely dated. Entries in **bold** are only for the reigns of emperors who controlled the greater part of the Empire.

BC	
753	Traditional date for foundation of Rome by Romulus.
509	Traditional date for expulsion of Rome's last king, Tarquinius Superbus.
496	Romans defeat the Latin League at the battle of Lake Regillus.
396	Veii falls after ten-year siege/blockade.
390	Gauls rout a Roman army at the River Allia and sack Rome.
343–341	First Samnite War.
340–338	Latin revolt defeated and Latin League dissolved.
326–304	Second Samnite War. Roman army defeated and sent under yoke at Caudine Forks (321).
298–290	Third Samnite War. Romans win major victory at Sentinum (295).
283	A Gallic tribe, the Boii, defeated at Lake Vadimo.
280–275	War with Pyrrhus, who defeats Romans at Heraclea (280) and Asculum (279), but is finally beaten at Malventum.
264–241	First Punic War.
260	Romans win naval victory off Mylae.
256	Major Roman naval victory off Ecnomus.
256–255	Regulus invades Africa, but after initial successes is defeated.
255–253	Roman fleets wrecked in storms off Pachynus and Palinurus.
249	Romans defeated in naval battle at Drepana.
241	Romans win final naval battle off the Aegates Islands.
225	Invading Gallic army defeated at Telamon.
223	Romans campaign successfully against tribes of Cisalpine Gaul.
218–201	Second Punic War.
218	Hannibal defeats cavalry force at Ticinus and then smashes two consular armies at Trebia.

217	Consul Flaminius is ambushed at Lake Trasimene.
216	Romans suffer massive defeat at Cannae.
214–205	First Macedonian War. Romans are forced to come to terms with Philip of Macedon after losing their allies in Greece.
213–211	Romans take Syracuse after long siege.
209	Scipio Africanus captures New Carthage.
208	Scipio wins a victory at Baecula.
207	Hasdrubal brings army into Italy but is defeated at Metaurus.
206	Scipio wins decisive victory in Spanish campaign at Ilipa.
204–203	Scipio invades Africa, winning battle of the Great Plains. Hannibal recalled.
202	Scipio defeats Hannibal at Zama.
200–196	Second Macedonian War.
197	Philip decisively beaten at Cynoscephalae.
197–179	Series of wars in Spain eventually ended by the campaigns and peace settlement of Gracchus.
192–189	Syrian War against the Seleucid Antiochus III.
191	Antiochus' invasion of Greece defeated at Thermopylae.
190	Antiochus defeated at Magnesia.
189–188	Manlius Vulso defeats Galatians.
172–167	Third Macedonian War.
168	Macedonians under Perseus defeated at Pydna.
154–138	Lusitanian War.
149–146	Third Punic War.
149–148	Fourth Macedonian War.
146	Destruction of Carthage and Corinth.
143–133	Numantine War.
125–121	Romans defeat tribes of Transalpine Gaul.
113–105	Migrating tribes, the Cimbri and Teutones, defeat a succession of Roman armies, culminating in the disaster at Arausio (105).
112–106	Jugurthine War begins with humiliating Roman surrender, but finally won by Marius.
102	Marius defeats Teutones at Aquae Sextiae.
101	Marius and Catulus defeat Cimbri at Vercellae.

91–88	The Social War, the last great rebellion by Rome's Italian allies is defeated after a hard struggle.
88	Sulla marches on Rome.
88–85	First Mithridatic War.
86	Sulla storms Athens and then defeats Mithridates' much larger armies at Chaeronea and Orchomenus.
83–82	Sulla returns to Italy and wins civil war at the battle of the Colline Gate outside Rome.
83–82	Second Mithridatic War.
82–72	Sertorius continues the civil war in Spain.
74–66	Third Mithridatic War.
73–70	A major slave rebellion led by Spartacus disrupts Italy. Several Roman armies are smashed before he is finally defeated by Crassus.
69	Lucullus defeats Tigranes of Armenia and captures his capital Tigranocerta.
68	Lucullus defeats combined forces of Tigranes and Mithridates at Tigranocerta.
67	Pompey clears the Mediterranean of pirates in a brief but highly organized campaign.
66	Pompey given extraordinary command to complete the war with Mithridates.
63	Pompey captures Jerusalem.
58–50	Caesar's conquest of Gallia Comata.
54–53	Crassus invades Parthia, but is defeated and killed at Carrhae.
52	Major Gallic rebellion led by Vercingetorix.
49–45	Civil War between Caesar and Pompey. Caesar wins victories at Pharsalus (48), Zela (47), Thapsus (46) and Munda (45).
44–42	Caesar's assassination provokes a further cycle of civil war between the conspirators and Caesar's supporters led by Mark Antony, later joined by Octavian, Caesar's nephew and adopted son.
42	Brutus and Cassius defeated in twin battles of Philippi.
40–38	Parthians invade Syria, but are defeated by Ventidius at Mt Amanus and Gindarus.
36	Antony launches major offensive against the Parthians, but this

	flounders when he fails to take Phraapsa, and he loses many men to disease and starvation in the subsequent retreat.
31	Antony defeated by Octavian in naval battle at Actium. Octavian becomes effectively the sole ruler of the Roman Empire.
31–30	Parthians overrun Armenia.
28–24	Final pacification of Spain completed by Octavian and his commanders.
27 BC–AD 14	**Principate of Augustus (Octavian).**
25	Successful expedition is sent against Ethiopia in response to raids on Roman Egypt.
20	Settlement with Parthia leads to the return of Roman prisoners and captured standards.
16–15	Campaigns to conquer the Alpine tribes.
15	German tribes raid the Roman provinces and defeat Lollius Urbicus.
12–7	Tiberius conquers Pannonia. He and his brother Drusus campaign in Germany.

AD

4–5	Tiberius completes the conquest of Germany as far as the Elbe.
6–9	Massive revolt in Pannonia and Dalmatia suppressed after hard struggle by Tiberius and Germanicus.
9	German revolt led by Arminius of the Cherusci massacres three legions under Varus in the Teutonberg Wald.
10–11	Tiberius and Germanicus secure the Rhine frontier.
14	Legions on Rhine and Danube mutiny after death of Augustus.
14–37	**Principate of Tiberius.**
15–16	Germanicus leads Rhine armies against the Germans and buries the remains of Varus' army. He defeats Arminius at Indistaviso, but fails to achieve final victory.
17–24	Revolt of Tacfarinas, a former auxiliary, in North Africa, which ends only when he is killed.
19	Arminius murdered by rival chieftains.
21	Revolt of Florus and Sacrovir in Gaul swiftly suppressed by Rhine armies.

28	The Frisii, a Germanic tribe east of the Rhine, rebel against oppressive taxation.
37–41	**Principate of Gaius (Caligula).**
40–44	Mauretania rebels and is fully conquered by Seutonius Paulinus and later Hosidius Geta.
41–54	**Principate of Claudius.**
42	Scribonius, the governor of Dalmatia, attempts a rebellion against Claudius, but commits suicide when his legions fail to support him.
43	Claudius launches invasion of Britain.
47	Corbulo suppresses the Frisii and defeats and kills the Chaucian Gannascus, a former auxiliary, who had been raiding the Roman provinces in a fleet of small ships.
51	Caratacus defeated, but the Silures of southern Wales continue to resist.
54–68	**Principate of Nero.**
58–64	War with Parthia over Armenia. Corbulo captures Artaxata and Tigranocerta.
60–61	Boudicca, Queen of the Iceni, leads rebellion in Britain, creating widespread devastation before she is defeated by Suetonius Paulinus.
62	Caesennius Paetus surrounded and surrenders to the Parthians, and his army is sent under the yoke.
66–74	The Jewish rebellion.
66	The Syrian governor, Cestius Gallus, leads an expedition to Jerusalem, but is forced to retreat and suffers heavily in the pursuit.
67	Vespasian subdues Galilee. Josephus surrenders to him.
68–9	Year of Four Emperors. Nero's death prompts a civil war as the provincial armies nominate their commanders as successor.
68	Emperor Galba murdered by his guardsmen after failing to meet their demands for pay. His successor, Otho, is defeated by Vitellius at the first battle of Cremona (or Bedriacum).
69	Supporters of Vespasian defeat Vitellius' army at the second battle of Cremona. Sarmatians and Dacians raid across the Danube.

69–70	In northern Germany a Batavian nobleman and former auxiliary prefect, Julius Civilis, leads a rebellion to create a 'Gallic empire'. He is defeated by Petilius Cerealis.
70–79	**Principate of Vespasian.**
70	Titus captures Jerusalem after a long siege.
73–4	Masada, the last stronghold of the Jewish rebels, is taken.
71–4	Petilius Cerealis defeats the Brigantes of northern Britain.
74–8	Julius Frontinus defeats the Silures of South Wales.
78–84	Julius Agricola advances into Scotland, defeating a large tribal army at Mons Graupius. His conquests are largely abandoned when troops are withdrawn to serve in the wars on the Danube.
79–81	**Principate of Titus.**
81–96	**Principate of Domitian.**
83	Domitian campaigns against the Chatti.
85	Decebalus, king of Dacia, invades Moesia and inflicts a heavy defeat on its governor.
86	Domitian's Praetorian Prefect, Cornelius Fuscus, is given command in Dacia, but is defeated and killed.
88	Another Roman army invades Dacia and defeats Decebalus at Tapae.
89	Saturninus, governor of Lower Germany, rebels against Domitian, but is defeated. Domitian makes peace with Decebalus, paying him a subsidy and providing technical experts to strengthen Dacia's fortresses. Sarmatian Iazyges raid Pannonia.
92	Further raids on Pannonia prompt Domitian to campaign against the Iazyges and their allies, the Marcomanni and Quadi.
96–8	**Principate of Nerva.**
98–117	**Principate of Trajan.**
101–2	Trajan's First Dacian War defeats Decebalus and removes the favourable Domitianic treaty.
105–6	Decebalus renews war but is defeated and commits suicide. Dacia is annexed as a province.
113–17	Trajan's Parthian War flounders when he fails to take Hatra. Revolts in recently conquered territory break out before his death.

115–17	Widespread rebellion by Jewish communities in Egypt, Cyrene and Cyprus.
117–38	**Principate of Hadrian**, during which Trajan's acquisitions in the East are abandoned.
122	Construction of Hadrian's Wall begins.
131–5	The Jews revolt under the Messianic leader, Bar Kochba, and are defeated at a heavy cost in Roman casualties.
138–61	**Principate of Antoninus Pius.**
138–9	Rebellion in northern Britain.
140–43	Antonine conquests in Scotland. Construction of Antonine Wall begins.
145	Rebellion in Mauretania.
c. 150–54	Serious rebellion in northern Britain. Antonine Wall abandoned. Hadrian's Wall reoccupied.
c. 160–63	Antonine Wall reoccupied and then evacuated again.
161–80	**Reign of Marcus Aurelius.**
162–6	Parthians invade Armenia. Lucius Verus, Marcus' Augustus or co-ruler, sent east to oppose them. They are defeated and Ctesiphon and Seleucia sacked.
167	Marcomanni and Quadi, two Suebic tribes, cross the Danube in a series of raids. One group reaches Aquileia in northern Italy. The Iazyges raid the province of Dacia.
168–75	A series of campaigns against the Marcomanni, Quadi and their Sarmatian allies.
175	Avidius Cassius, the governor of Syria, rebels on receiving a false report of Marcus' death, but is defeated by loyal troops.
178–80	Further disturbances on the Danube.
180–92	**Reign of Commodus.**
c. 182–5	Heavy fighting in northern Britain eventually ended by victories of Ulpius Marcellus.
184	Final abandonment of Antonine Wall.
193–7	Period of civil war results from murder of Commodus. It is eventually won by Septimius Severus supported by the Danubian armies.
197–208	**Reign of Severus.**
198	Severus invades Parthia and sacks Ctesiphon.

205	Hadrian's Wall restored after heavy raids by Caledonian tribes had overrun much of northern Britain.
208–11	Severus leads large expedition against the Caledonians, but dies in Eboracum (York).
211–17	**Caracalla's reign.**
213	Caracalla campaigns on the Rhine frontier.
217	Caracalla prepares eastern expedition, but is murdered by a member of his Horse Guards near Carrhae.
217–18	**Macrinus' reign.** He is defeated by Persians at Nisibis, and then by the usurper Elagabalus outside Antioch.
218–22	**Reign of Elagabalus.**
227	Ardashir defeats Parthian king and creates Sassanid monarchy.
222–35	**Reign of Severus Alexander.**
230	Persians invade Mesopotamia and besiege Nisibis.
232	Severus Alexander's offensive against the Persians fails.
234–5	Pannonian legions rebel under Maximinus. Severus is murdered.
235–8	**Reign of Maximinus,** who campaigns successfully against the Alamanni but is murdered by the Praetorian Guard.
238–44	**Reign of Gordian III.**
242	Successful expedition to drive Persians from Mesopotamia.
244	Gordian III murdered by a conspiracy and replaced by Philip, the Praetorian Prefect.
244–9	**Reign of Philip the Arab.**
245–7	Gothic tribes raid Danubian provinces.
249	Decius is proclaimed emperor by the Danubian armies and defeats Philip near Verona. Goths under Cniva raid Danubian provinces.
249–51	**Reign of Decius.**
251	Decius defeated and killed by Goths at Forum Trebonii.
251–3	**Reign of Gallus.**
252	Persians invade Mesopotamia. Heavy barbarian raiding across Rhine and Danube. Goths paid a subsidy to withdraw.
253	Aemilianus rebels at head of Pannonian and Moesian armies. Gallus' army deserts and murders him. Aemilianus is then murdered by his own troops.

253–60	**Reign of Valerian.** His son Gallienus made Augustus.
254	Marcomanni launch heavy raids into Illyricum. Goths raid Thrace. Shapur I of Persia captures Nisibis.
256	Franks launch heavy raids across Lower Rhine. Gothic fleet raids coast of Asia Minor causing widespread devastation and panic.
258/9	Gallienus defeats Franks.
260	Valerian's Persian expedition ends in disaster when he surrenders to Sharpur. Postumus proclaimed emperor in Gaul, creating the *imperium Gallicum* with a capital at Trier which lasts a decade.
260–68	**Reign of Gallienus.**
261	Odenathus of Palmyra made *dux orientis* and leads successful war against the Persians.
267–8	Odenathus murdered. His power assumed by his widow, Zenobia, in the name of their son Vallabathus.
268	Goths raid Thrace and Greece. The Heruli sack Athens. Gallienus defeats the Heruli near the River Nessus, but is murdered by his own officers.
268–70	**Reign of Claudius II 'Gothicus'.**
269	Claudius defeats Goths in great victory at Naissus. Zenobia captures Antioch.
270	Claudius dies of disease and is succeeded by Aurelian. Dacia abandoned.
270–75	**Reign of Aurelian.**
270–71	Aurelian defeats Juthungi and Vandals. Zenobia takes Egypt and invades Asia Minor.
272–3	Aurelian defeats Zenobia at Antioch and Emesa. Palmyra destroyed and Egyptian revolt suppressed.
274	Tetricus rebels in Gaul and is defeated by Aurelian.
275	Aurelian is murdered by his own officers. Tacitus made emperor by the Senate.
276	Tacitus defeats Alans, but dies on campaign.
276–82	**Reign of Probus.** He campaigns successfully on the Rhine and Danube, but is murdered by mutinous soldiers and replaced by Carus, the Praetorian Prefect.

283–5	Carus defeats Sarmatians in Illyricum, but dies during a successful offensive against Persia. Civil war eventually won by Diocletian who appoints Maximian as his Caesar and later as Augustus.
284–305	**Reign of Diocletian**, which saw the creation of the Tetrarchy.
286	Maximian suppresses the Bagaudaen disturbances in Gaul, which had escalated from banditry to full-scale revolt.
286–93	Maximian fights a successful campaign against the Alamanni. Carausius leads a successful rebellion in Britain but is eventually murdered.
296–7	Diocletian suppresses usurpation in Egypt. Constantius regains Britain. Galerius defeats the Persians.
305–23	Period of civil wars following the abdication of Diocletian and Maximian.
305	Constantius campaigns against Caledonians.
306	Constantius dies in York and his son Constantine is proclaimed emperor by the provincial army.
312	Constantine defeats Maxentius at the Milvian Bridge outside Rome.
314–15	Constantine wins victories at Cibalis and Mardia in civil war with Licinius.
322–3	Constantine campaigns against Sarmatians and Goths on the Danube.
323–4	Constantine decisively defeats Licinius at Adrianople and Chrysopolis.
324–37	**Reign of Constantine** as undisputed emperor.
331–4	Constantine successfully campaigns against the Goths and Sarmatians.
337	Imperial power divided between Constantine's sons.
337–60	War with Persia.
338	Persians mount unsuccessful siege of Nisibis.
340–69	Severe problems in Britain. Heavy raiding by barbarians.
346	Persians mount unsuccessful siege of Nisibis.
348	Persians defeat Constantius at Singara.
350–53	Persians again fail to take Nisibis. Civil war between Constantius and Magnentius.

356–7	Julian campaigns against the Alamanni, winning a pitched battle at Strasbourg.
357–9	Constantius defeats the Quadi and Sarmatians who had made heavy raids into the Danubian provinces.
358	Julian campaigns against the Franks.
359	Persians invade Mesopotamia and take Amida by storm.
360	The Persians take Singara. Germanic tribes make deep raids into Gaul. Picts and Scots launch heavy raids into Britain.
360–61	Julian campaigns across the Rhine. Death of Constantius.
363	Julian Persian offensive ends in disaster and he is killed in a skirmish. Jovian agrees humiliating peace with Persia, ceding them considerable territory including Nisibis.
366–9	Valentinian campaigns against Alamanni and beyond the Rhine against the Goths.
367–9	Roman army under the *comes*, Theodosius restores order in Britain. Valentinian campaigns against the Alamanni while Valens defeats the Goths.
371–5	Valentian formally receives a group of Alamanni into the Empire. Rebellion in Mauretania suppressed by Theodosius.
375	Valentinian dies of apoplexy while haranguing some Quadic chieftains.
376–7	A party of Goths fleeing Hunnic attacks cross the Danube and defeat Romans near Salices.
378	Alamanni attack Raetia. Valens is defeated and killed along with most of his army by the Goths at Adrianople.
380–82	Successful operations against the Goths.
383	Magnus Maximus defeats Picts, but then rebels.
388	Theodosius defeats Magnus Maximus. Valentinian II is undisputed western emperor until his death (392).
394	Theodosius defeats rivals in costly two-day battle at the River Frigidus.
395–400	Theodosius' death prompts renewed civil war.
398–400	Victories in northern Britain over Picts, Scots and Saxons.
407	Army in Britain raises Constantine III to the throne and invades Gaul, fighting against Vandals.
408	Goths under Alaric invade Italy and besiege Rome.

409	Britain rebels against Constantine III.
410	Alaric sacks Rome.
415	Visigoths are sent by Constantius to Spain to fight against Vandals.
418	Visigoths are settled by Constantius in Aquitaine.
429	Vandals invade and overrun Africa.
451–3	Aetius turns back the offensive of Attila's Huns at Chalons (Campus Mauriacus). Attila bribed to withdraw from Italy and dies soon afterwards.
454	Ostrogoths settle in Pannonia.
469–78	Visigoths overrun Spain.
476	Last emperor of the West, Romulus Augustus, deposed by Odovacer who creates the Ostrogothic kingdom of Italy.
502–6	Anastasian war with Persia. Persians capture Amida, but this is returned to Romans as part of the peace treaty.
526–32	Renewal of war with Persia.
528	Belisarius defeated at Minduos.
530	Belisarius wins great victory at Dara.
531	Belisarius defeated at Callinicum.
533–4	Belisarius defeats Vandals in Africa.
535–54	Attempt made to reconquer Italy with armies led by Belisarius and later Narses. Rome captured and recaptured several times. Narses defeats the Goths at Taginae (552) and Vesuvius (553), and the Franks at Casilinus (554).

INTRODUCTION

To Overcome the Proud in War

This mosaic pavement dates to the first or second century AD and depicts a group of soldiers in either an historical or mythical scene. Their uniforms are highly romanticized. The evidence for the colour of Roman soldiers' tunics is inconclusive, but suggests that in most periods these were white, or off-white as shown here.

Introduction

WARFARE PLAYED A major part throughout Rome's history, creating and maintaining an empire which eventually included much of Europe, the Near East and North Africa. War and politics were inseparably linked at Rome, and the right to exercise power in peacetime was purchased by the obligation to provide successful leadership in war. The Latin word *imperator*, from which we derive 'emperor', means general, and even the least military of emperors paraded the martial successes achieved by their armies. The willingness of Roman soldiers to fight each other made possible the cycles of civil wars that caused the collapse of the Republican system of government in the first century BC and prompted the fragmentation of imperial power in the third century AD. In spite of the importance of warfare, Roman society gradually became largely demilitarized. The citizen militia, recruited from the property owners serving out of duty to the state and not for pay or booty, was replaced by a professional army drawn mainly from the poorest elements in society. By the second century AD only a tiny minority of soldiers, even in the citizen legions, had been born in Italy. For a while the senatorial and equestrian officers, who filled the senior ranks as part of a career including both civil and military posts, provided a link between the army and the rest of society, but this was largely severed in the third century. After this both officers and men were career soldiers with aspirations clearly distinct from the lives of civilians in the provinces.

Roman warfare was characterized by great ferocity and the Roman pursuit of victory was relentless. Tacitus makes a Caledonian war leader claim that the Romans 'create a desolation, and call it peace'. The Romans had a pragmatic attitude towards atrocity and massacre that viewed almost any act as justifiable if it eased the path to victory. The Roman sack of a city which had failed to surrender before the first battering-ram touched the wall was deliberately made appalling to deter resistance elsewhere. Rebellions in particular were suppressed with great brutality and frequently involved the mass crucifixion of prisoners or their violent deaths on the sand of the arena. But against the destructiveness and ferocity of Roman wars must be set their often constructive results. The Romans profited from many of their wars, especially in the period of conquest, but their war making was never purely predatory. Defeated enemies were turned into subordinate allies who soon provided many loyal soldiers to fight the next generation of Rome's wars. Gradually some of their former enemies gained Roman citizenship and might even in time gain admission to the élite of the Empire. Roman rule was imposed and maintained by force, but it inaugurated in most areas periods of peace and prosperity far greater than was enjoyed in the centuries before or after the Empire. Despite the claims of some authors writing at the height of the Empire's power, the Romans had not acquired their Empire out of a sense of duty to organize

Roman legionaries employ the famous tortoise (testudo) formation, in an attack on a Dacian stronghold. Their long rectangular shields were overlapped to form a continuous roof above their heads. Only the heaviest missiles were capable of penetrating a well-formed tortoise and we hear of one incident where the defenders toppled a heavy catapult over the wall to crush the roof of shields.

and administer the provincials for their own good, but out of a self-interested desire for profit and glory. Once a people had fought against Rome then they would always be viewed as a potential enemy until they had ceased to possess the capacity to wage war against her. The simplest and most effective way of achieving this was to absorb them as a clearly subordinate ally or dependent province. The Romans displayed a talent for absorbing former enemies that was unique in the ancient world.

The professional Roman army was the most advanced fighting force that the world had ever seen. A comparable force was not to emerge in Europe for well over a thousand years after Rome's fall. In many respects it was surprisingly modern, with its emphasis on uniform, drill and clearly defined unit organization and command structure. Soldiers followed a well-defined career pattern, they were paid at a standard rate subject to various deductions, and their whole lives regulated and recorded by a complex military bureaucracy. Many

aspects of the life and daily routine of the Roman army would be instantly familiar to modern soldiers. However, it is important to remember that in other respects its behaviour was distinctively Roman and reflected the society which produced it. The origins of the army in a citizens' militia, in which the whole community served in differing capacities according to their age and status, left a sense of shared endeavour, and allowed Roman soldiers a freedom to express their opinion to their commanders which sometimes seems at odds with the army's harsh discipline. Promotion in the army was based primarily on patronage, with merit and seniority playing a subsidiary role. While patronage may in practice be common in many modern institutions, including armies, it is normally seen as a corruption of the proper, fair system of promotion. For the Romans patronage was not a corruption of a fairer system; it was the system and was openly accepted as a part of normal life.

The Roman bridge at Merida still crosses the wide River Guadiana on sixty arches. The Roman city of Augusta Emerita was founded by Augustus as a colony for veterans from two of his legions. Many of the great architectural projects throughout the Empire were undertaken or supervised by military engineers.

The Romans are often seen as a methodical and highly practical people whose feats of engineering allowed their army to operate more efficiently. Roman roads, perhaps the most famous of all their legacies, provided direct, well-maintained routes along which the army could supply its garrisons or shift reserves in all but the worst of weather conditions. They were also deliberately built on a monumental scale in obsessively straight lines to be a spectacular statement of power. The bridges which, at the start of a campaign, the army was willing to build with great labour across wide rivers like the Rhine and Danube, served the practical purpose of allowing the army to cross, but were also indicative of the Romans' ability to overcome nature itself as well as any enemy.

The marching camp, built at the end of each day's march to a standard pattern, offered security for the night to the soldiers and their baggage. Its highly regimented appearance and the construction of a fresh camp after each day's advance were highly intimidating, emphasizing the steady, relentless advance of the army. The Roman genius was to combine the practical with the visually spectacular, so that the army's actions were often designed to overawe the enemy with a display of massive power before they actually reached him.

THE DEVELOPMENT OF WARFARE

This volume is about Roman warfare, but there are many aspects which it cannot hope to cover in any detail. It would be impossible in the space available to provide a detailed narrative of all the wars fought by Rome from the foundation of the city to the sixth century AD. Instead I have tried to trace the development of warfare within the context of the evolution of the army and state, or at least in the case of the latter those aspects of politics and society connected with the military. The nature of the army, why and with what objectives it fought a war, and the way in which it operated are discussed for each period and placed in the context of the military institutions of the main opponents faced in each period. This cannot hope to be a full history of the Roman army since

The amphitheatre at Merida could seat around 15,000 spectators to watch the gladiatorial fights staged in its arena. This is just one of hundreds of spectacular monuments still to be seen on the sites of cities throughout the Roman Empire in the provinces conquered and defended by the Roman army.

many aspects, such as its equipment, career and service patterns, pay and daily routine, its role in the administration of the provinces, or the layout of its forts and bases, can only be dealt with very briefly. The bibliography lists, for each chapter, modern works that deal with the issues discussed and other aspects of the army in this period. The list is not exhaustive and has been restricted to works in English, since a full list of works on the Roman army would be truly massive. Combined with the bibliographies of the works mentioned, however, it should provide a starting point for personal study into any more specific topic. There is also a section listing the main Greek and Latin sources for the period, discussing briefly their style, reliability and usefulness. Most are available in translation and will be essential reading for a deeper understanding of Roman warfare.

CHAPTER ONE.

Early Rome
and the
Conquest
of Italy

*These two bone plaques from Praeneste are
decorated with pictures of Italian hoplites.
Each man wears a crested helmet, muscled
cuirass (probably in bronze), greaves, tunic
and cloak. They each hold a spear and have
a round shield, the heavy* hoplon, *resting
against their legs. None of this equipment
would have been out of place in the phalanxes
of Classical Greece.*

Early Rome and the Conquest of Italy

THE ROMANS' OWN MYTHS concerning their origins were dominated by tales of war tinged with a good deal of pure savagery. Romulus and Remus, the twin sons of the war god Mars, were suckled by a she-wolf and as adults gathered a warrior band which supported itself by raiding. The foundation of the city was stained by fratricide when Romulus killed his brother in a fit of rage. Throughout his life Romulus remained the heroic war leader, justifying his right to rule by his conspicuous courage and prowess in battle. The majority of the tales of Rome's early years recounted heroism in war. It is impossible now to know just how much, if any, truth is contained in these stories. The Romans themselves did not begin to write history until the end of the third century BC and preserved very little reliable information concerning earlier events. By that time Rome was already firmly established as the dominant power in Italy and had begun to enter the world stage. The warfare which formed a major part of her rise to this position is the subject of this chapter, but it is important to remember how poor the sources for this period are.

Traditionally Rome was founded in 753 BC, although archaeology has revealed traces of settlements near what would become the site of the future city from the beginning of the

When the Romans began to record their own history in the later third century BC they had only the haziest knowledge of their city's origins. By this time the story of Romulus founding Rome after the murder of his twin brother Remus was the most common, but not the only, version of these events.

last millennium BC. The merging of several of these villages into a single settlement that could be called a city did not occur until the sixth century BC. The site is a good one, with easily defensible hills next to a natural crossing place of the River Tiber, and commanding traditional trade routes into central Italy, including the Via Salaria, the Salt Road running from the coast. Rome was just one of several Latin communities occupying an area of the coastal plain west of the Apennines, the line of hills which forms the spine of Italy. Sixth-century Rome may well have been the largest of all the Latin cities, but it is unclear whether it was also the most powerful.

The wars fought by early Rome consisted of small-scale raids and cattle rustling, with perhaps the occasional ritualized battle. The 'armies' were warrior bands formed by an aristocrat, his kin and dependants. The leaders were not commanders with formal powers but heroes who led by personal example, fighting as conspicuously as possible in advance of their followers. The leader fought for personal glory, the followers out of loyalty to the leader who provided for them. The successful leader was the man who could protect his dependants from the depredations of other warrior bands and provide enough booty to satisfy his followers. This type of warfare has much in common with that described in Homer's poems and was probably prevalent in most of the 'barbarian' societies of western Europe at this period.

A major development came with the adoption of the hoplite phalanx, probably some time in the sixth century. Hoplite warfare developed in early seventh-century Greece and may well have spread to Italy via the Greek colonies of the southern peninsula. A hoplite was a spearman, heavily protected by a bronze helmet, cuirass, greaves, and a circular, bronze-covered shield, 90 centimetres (3 feet) in diameter. Hoplites fought as a group, not as individuals. Advancing in a densely packed phalanx, normally at least eight ranks deep, hoplites could expect to drive back most opposition. Individual weapon skills were less important for a hoplite than maintaining the cohesion of the phalanx. Hoplite warfare required little formal training or discipline, but it demanded a new military ethos. It was no longer possible for aristocratic warriors to range around a battlefield, entering and leaving combat as the mood took them, singling out only those opponents they considered worthy of their attentions, and with their main concern the acquisition of personal honour. Hoplites depended on the men on either side of them staying in position, in particular on the man to their right offering some protection to their vulnerable unshielded side.

The rise of the hoplite was associated with social change and the rise of the city state, broadening participation in combat beyond the aristocracy and their followers. Hoplites were drawn from those able to afford the necessary equipment, and as cities developed and prospered this came to include a much higher proportion of the population, consisting primarily of farmers. Such men were expected to fight harder for the state, since as men of property they had an interest in its preservation. They gained increased political power within the city, earning these rights through their obligation to fight to protect the community. This was the ideal of the citizen soldier, the man who fought not for pay, booty or glory, but out of civic duty. The domination of the hoplite class by small farmers gave hoplite warfare, at least in Greece, a peculiar rhythm of its own, fitting in with the agricultural year. Prolonged campaigning kept a farmer away from his fields when they most needed his attention, so wars tended to consist of a single day of battle between two phalanxes. Battles were usually provoked by a symbolic devastation of the enemy's fields which inflicted little actual damage. The rituals of hoplite warfare in Greece were those of the state, not of the aristocratic war leader and his warrior band. The community formed by the hoplite class was the dominant force in politics as it was the basis of the army in war.

Two of our main sources for this period, Livy and Dionysius, attributed a major reform of Rome's political, social and military organization to Servius Tullius (traditionally 579–534 BC). The reform was linked to hoplite warfare and as the archaeological record suggests that hoplite equipment was adopted in the sixth century, the tradition may be broadly accurate. The Servian constitution divided the population into classes based on an assessment of their property, each class providing itself with a specified set of equipment – a full hoplite panoply for Class I, to just a sling for Class V. This system provided the basis of the *Comitia Centuriata*, the voting assembly at which the people elected consuls and declared wars until the end of the Republic, so our sources may have been attempting to reconstruct the original reform from their knowledge of the later political system. The *Comitia Centuriata* met on the Campus Martius, the Plain of Mars, outside the boundary of the city, where the army had always mustered, since citizens were barred from carrying weapons inside the city. Its structure exemplified the ideal of a citizen militia, men voting and fighting together in the same units. By the late Republic the centuries in the assembly were not of a standard size, but it seems logical that originally they had consisted of about a hundred men. The presence of three distinct types of heavy infantry was probably influenced by the knowledge that the later manipular legion fought in three lines. It is unlikely that this degree of tactical sophistication was present at such an early stage in the army's development. More probably the original Servian reform was much simpler and the main distinction was between those able to equip themselves as hoplites and the more numerous remainder who took the field only as light infantry or servants. The former were known as the *classis*, the remainder *infra classem*. The original *classis* probably consisted of Class I, possibly in forty centuries of around a hundred men, which might suggest that sixth-century Rome could potentially muster a phalanx of four thousand men, a not impossible figure given the size of the city suggested by the archaeological evidence. At some later date as the city grew in size, Classes II and III were able to afford heavier equipment and were admitted to the phalanx, their twenty centuries increasing the number of hoplites to six thousand. This reconstruction remains conjectural.

The seventh-century BC Chigi vase was one of very few attempts by Greek artists to represent hoplite phalanxes in battle. Men are shown advancing to the accompaniment of a flute player towards a similarly equipped enemy phalanx coming towards them. Like the later makers of the Bayeux tapestry, the vase painters encountered the problem of depicting a formation which was both wide and deep in a two-dimensional medium. Their solution was the same, to show the figures one behind the other, closely overlapping.

THE REPUBLIC

The expulsion of the kings from Rome may well have been part of a wider series of political and social upheavals that occurred throughout late sixth-century Latium and Etruria. At the battle of Lake Regillus (496 BC), the army of the young Republic faced a Latin army, traditionally including the supporters of the expelled Tarquins. Livy and Dionysius both considered this to have been a battle between phalanxes, although their accounts have a distinctly heroic quality. The Roman Republic possessed a hoplite phalanx and did fight pitched battles, but not all its wars conformed to the rigid pattern of hoplite warfare in contemporary Greece. The Roman cavalry seems to have played a greater role than was the case with most Greek armies, although on at least some occasions horsemen may have dismounted and joined the phalanx. Our sources depict most of the campaigns between Rome and her neighbours as little more than raids, yet such frequent raiding was anathema to the hoplite mentality. In 479 BC Rome was faced by small-scale raiding from neighbouring Veii. The clan of the Fabii, led by one of their number who was the consul in that year, approached the Senate and offered to wage the war against Veii as a private struggle, prosecuted solely by themselves, their retainers and dependants. Stationing themselves on the borders, the 306 Fabii patrolled against Etruscan raids and in turn raided the enemy. They were ambushed and wiped out while on a cattle raid, only one Fabius surviving to carry on the family name. If the episode is genuine (it is possible that it was invented by later Roman writers to provide a heroic incident mirroring the last stand of the three hundred Spartans of Leonidas in 480 BC), then it appears to have more in common with the behaviour of the aristocratic warrior bands which it is thought the hoplite phalanx had superseded. However, the lands of the Fabii do appear to have been situated on the border with Veii, and it may be significant that the Fabii disappear from the *Fasti*, the official lists of magistrates, for the following twelve years.

A striking feature of this incident and many other campaigns was the central importance of the acquisition of booty. This seems to have been a major motivation for Roman soldiers and disputes over the distribution of the spoils were a common cause of dissent in the army. Many of the earliest recorded treaties between Rome and other states included clauses precisely detailing the entitlement to spoils in any conflict.

Rome possessed a phalanx in the sixth and fifth centuries BC, but most of her military activity consisted of raiding or reacting to enemy raids, types of fighting for which a phalanx was completely unsuited. Conflict between Rome and her neighbours varied in scale from minor theft or destruction of property to a full-scale pitched battle when two phalanxes confronted each other. Warfare might be waged by the whole populace under arms led by the elected magistrates of the state or just by individual clans or families following their allegiance to the aristocracy. Rome possessed a college of priests known as the *fetiales* who oversaw the justice of disputes with groups outside the community. When these had decided that a neighbour had committed such great offences against Rome that war was necessary, a representative of the college would enter enemy territory and present a list of grievances which, if redress was not made within thirty days, would result in the declaration of war. If the enemy failed to make satisfactory recompense then war was formally declared by the ritual of a fetial hurling a spear into enemy territory. This process has been taken to signify that the Romans had a very clear idea of the distinction between a state of war and peace with their neighbours, but it may have more to do with different types of hostility. The fetials, and the other similar priestly colleges in Latin and Etruscan cities, seem to have regulated the scale and limits of war between their communities, deciding when provocation required a response and what the size of that response should be, and controlling the escalation of conflict from private to state level. Anthropologists studying the warfare of primitive peoples in more recent times have discovered similar patterns where distinct levels of fighting, from ritualized duelling, through raiding to full-scale battles, occur depending on the situation. It is important to remember how small scale all of Rome's military activity was in this period. Her own territories and population were not large and the neighbours, which she raided and was in turn raided by on such a regular basis, were often less than a day's journey away. It is sobering to remember that the city of Veii, with which Rome fought a series of wars spanning a century, was situated not much more than 15 kilometres away.

Veii was captured in 396 BC after a long siege, the first time that the Romans ever paid their citizen soldiers. Veii's territory was annexed and much of the land settled by Roman citizens. The warfare of the late fifth and fourth centuries BC became increasingly bitter and the consequences for the losers much more serious. The peoples of the coastal plain were under great pressure from the expanding population of the Sabellian tribes of the Apennines. In the 420s BC these invaders swept through the fertile Campanian Plain taking Capua and Cumae. Further south another Sabellian people, the Lucanians, drove into the territories of the Greek coastal cities, while the Samnites established themselves in central Italy. Gallic tribes pushed down from the north, putting particular pressure on the northern Etruscan cities. In 390 BC a raiding band of Gauls, perhaps on their way to seek mercenary service in southern Italy or Sicily, routed a Roman army on the banks of the River Allia outside Rome. The Gauls sacked Rome, forcing the few defenders of the Capitol to buy their safety with a colossal bribe of gold. When the Romans complained that the Gauls were using crooked weighing scales to enlarge the agreed sum, the Gallic leader threw his sword on to the scales with the stern words, 'Vae Victis!', 'Woe to the defeated!' This is just one of the myths that grew up surrounding the Gallic sack. Others tales did more to salve Rome's pride, such as the story of the sacred geese of Juno Sospita whose cackling warned the defenders of the Capitol of a Gallic attack and allowed them to defeat it, or the exiled general Camillus, who returned at the eleventh hour to crush the raiders just as they were receiving their gold. In practical terms the damage inflicted by the Gauls was relatively small and soon repaired, since they

The Gallic sack of Rome in 390 BC had little long-term effect on the city's growth, but left a deep scar on the Roman psyche. Later tradition claimed that a band of defenders had held out on the Capitol, managing to repulse a Gallic night attack when they were woken by the cackling of the geese kept in Juno's Temple.

do not seem to have stayed in the city for any length of time or carried out any systematic destruction. However, the trauma of the Gallic sack left a legacy of fear and hatred of the northern barbarians, and may in the short term have increased the Romans' sense of vulnerability.

The story of Rome's early history is one of steady, if often slow, growth in power and size. The earliest myths of Rome's history show a willingness to absorb outsiders into the community, an attitude quite unlike that of most Greek city states who were highly jealous of the privileges of citizenship. Slaves, most of whom at this period were war captives, received full citizen rights when they gained their freedom. Some entire Latin communities were absorbed into the citizen body, while others received more limited rights of commerce with Roman citizens without gaining the full franchise. This produced a steady increase in the available citizen manpower and fostered military success. Defeated enemy communities were turned into allies who provided troops to serve Rome in future campaigns. In some cases conquered territory was settled with colonies composed of both Romans and Latins, establishing cities which not only helped to defend the gains, but also provided an additional source of military manpower for the future. In this way, and also through receiving a portion of the spoils, Rome's allies shared in her successes. They were not equal partners, but nor were they entirely unwilling. Latin rebellions against Rome became less and less common and seldom united more than a few communities. The last serious revolt occurred in the 340s BC, but only a proportion of the Latin cities took part and by this time Rome had become so strong that her eventual success was never in doubt.

The steady growth in Rome's military manpower gave her great advantages over other peoples, so that a sizeable field army needed to consist of only a proportion of the available citizen manpower. Such an army could afford to stay in the field for a longer period without this causing catastrophic damage to the community's economy and bringing on famine. This, and the ability to accept higher losses than they had previously, permitted Roman warfare to become both more determined and more decisive. It also began to change the army into something more sophisticated than a simple citizen militia. The word *legio*, or legion, literally meant 'levy' and seems at first to have been a name for the entire army of the Roman people. At some stage the single levy of six thousand heavy infantry was divided into two separate legions, presumably of half this size. This change may have been associated with the fall of the monarchy, providing each of the two annually elected consuls of the Republic with an army. It is doubtful that the full levy was called out for most of the small raids which still formed the greatest part of warfare.

The Republic also experimented with other colleges of senior magistrates. In several years between three and six tribunes with consular powers were elected instead of the consuls. This reform was primarily caused by the political disputes between the patrician aristocracy and the increasingly wealthy plebeians who formed the rest of the citizen body, but may also have reflected a military requirement

The Roman conquest of Italy

Rome had gradually grown in size from its earliest history, absorbing other peoples into the population, but it was only in the second half of the fourth century that her expansion began in earnest. Then, in less than a hundred years, the Romans defeated the Samnites, Etruscans, the Gallic tribes south of the Po and, finally, the peoples of southern Italy. Some land was confiscated from the defeated peoples and used to establish colonies of Roman and Latin citizens, which acted as garrisons in each area. However, in most cases the conquered states were absorbed into Rome's network of allies and in their turn provided soldiers to fight in Rome's next round of conquests.

Rome in the late Republic

(1) Templum Jovi Capitolini

(2) Comitium with Curia Hostilia

(3) Basilica Aemilia

(4) Tabularium

(5) Basilica Julia

(6) Forum Julium

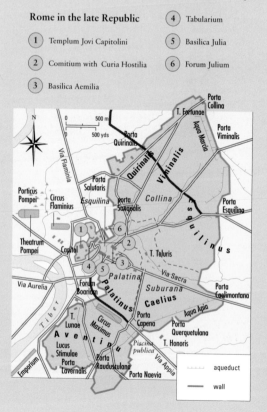

Roman conquest of Italy
265 BC

- Roman territory in 298 BC
- Samnite League 298 BC
- annexed by Rome 263 BC
- Roman colonies by 272 BC
- under Roman control by 270 BC
- Carthaginian possessions c. 260 BC

AULS

Ariminum

Ager Gallicum

Arretium

Sentinum

Ancona

Volaterrae

Picenum

A d r i a t i c

Etruria

Umbria

Aurinia

Volsinii

Asculum

Hadria

Cosa

Nepet

SABINES

S e a

Volci

Falerii

AEQUI

MARRUCINI

Caere

Tibur

Alba Fucens

FRENTANI

MARSI PAELIGNI

Ostia

Rome

Praeneste

Latium

Interamna

Lucera

Arpino

Tarracina

A p u l i a

Camusium

Suessa

Saticula

Barium

Capua

Benevebtum

Venusia

Cumae

Campania

Neapolis

Brundisium

Tyrrhenian

Lucania

Tarentum

Sea

Metapontum

Sinus

Tarentinus

Thurii

Croton

Bruttium

Panormus

Locri

Lilybaeum

Rhegium

Syracuse

0   50 km

0   50 miles

N

12°   16°

to field a number of smaller forces instead of two large armies. In years of particularly fierce political dissension or military crisis a dictator was appointed, exercising supreme authority for the six-month duration of his office. This was a more effective method of fielding a single, combined army than expecting two consuls with equal authority to work together. One of Rome's most cherished stories was that of Lucius Quinctius Cincinnatus, the senator called from the plough to become dictator and save the city when the army had been surrounded and trapped by the Aequi. Cincinnatus raised another levy, defeated the Aequi and rescued the army, returned to Rome to celebrate a triumph and resigned the dictatorship after fifteen days to return to working his fields. It was the classic example of selfless devotion to the state. It is a striking indication of the importance of the heavy infantry hoplites that a dictator was not allowed to lead his army on horseback. His subordinate, the *magister equitum*, or Master of Horse, led the cavalry, while the dictator stayed with the main phalanx.

The organization of the legions started to become more formal in the second half of the fourth century BC, as wars tended to consist less often of raiding and increasingly frequently of larger operations. Each legion was commanded by six military tribunes, elected by the people after 311 BC. From at least this date there were normally four legions raised in each year, so that the standard consular army consisted of two legions. Its internal organization became more important and the crude tactics of the phalanx were replaced by the more flexible manipular system, the legion deploying in three lines instead of one, each line consisting of small, independent units, maniples of two centuries. The manipular legion will be discussed in detail in the next chapter. Its introduction may well have been learned through experience, fighting in the rough terrain of the Apennines during the three great Samnite wars (343–290 BC).

The conflict with the Samnite confederation was Rome's last great struggle against an Italian opponent. In 321 BC the Samnites inflicted a disaster on the Romans to rank alongside the Allia rout, when a Roman army surrendered at the Caudine Forks. The Romans suffered the humiliation of being forced to walk underneath a yoke of spears, an act symbolizing their loss of warrior status. This defeat was to be the last in which Rome accepted unfavourable peace terms and acknowledged the loss of a war. It was five years before she renewed the struggle. In 295 BC the Romans achieved a great victory when both consuls took the field with a combined force of four legions. During the battle one of the consuls, Publius Decius Mus, made a formal *devotio*, pledging to sacrifice both himself and the enemy armies to Mother Earth and the gods of the Underworld in return for victory, before plunging to his death in the thick of the fray. It was an action his father is said to have performed in battle against the Latin rebels at Veseris in 340 BC. The behaviour of the Roman aristocracy still showed some traces of primitive heroic culture.

By the beginning of the third century BC Rome was without doubt the strongest power in Italy. As Rome had developed from small settlements to a great city possessing a large citizen population and controlling a large territory, so its warfare had changed from the ritual battles and minor depredations of aristocratic warrior bands into the larger scale, more concerted campaigns of an army organized, paid and controlled by the state. These armies were capable of forcing states to become permanent subordinate allies of Rome or, alternatively, of destroying them.

Roman warfare was capable of inflicting far more permanent damage on an enemy, but while it had become more destructive we should never ignore the constructive nature of Roman war making. Rome's allies were tied to her by very strong bonds and if her rule was not entirely benevolent, nor was it entirely repressive, the allies also benefiting from future successful wars. Each was tied more to Rome than to each other. The cohesiveness of the network of allies constructed by Rome around herself was to be demonstrated by the succession of major conflicts fought against foreign powers in the third century BC. Despite the many heavy losses suffered by Rome, very few of her allies responded to her opponents' blandishments and defected.

CHAPTER TWO

The Wars with Carthage and the Hellenistic Kingdoms

This plate from Campania is decorated with a picture of a war elephant followed by a calf and may show one of the animals brought by King Pyrrhus of Epirus when he fought against Rome on behalf of the city for Tarentum. This was the first time that the Romans had faced war elephants, and the animals played a major part in Pyrrhus' victories. However, they were liable to panic, stampeding in all directions, and often caused as much damage to their own side as the enemy. This animal is clearly an Indian elephant and is crewed by a mahout or driver and two javelinmen in the tower carried on the animal's back. Notice the goad carried by the mahout, who in some cases was equipped with a hammer and a chisel-like blade, which he was supposed to drive into the animal's spine if it began to panic. Hasdrubal, the brother of Hannibal was credited with the invention of this device.

The Wars with Carthage and the Hellenistic Kingdoms

IN 281 BC THE GREEK city of Tarentum in southern Italy called on King Pyrrhus of Epirus for assistance in its war with Rome. Pyrrhus was the greatest soldier of his day, raised in the hard school of the decades of warfare which followed the death of Alexander the Great and the break-up of his short-lived empire. He was something of a scientific soldier, producing several works of military theory, but in battle he led as Alexander had done, charging spear in hand at the head of his élite cavalry. When he landed in Italy Pyrrhus brought with him an army of well-trained professional soldiers, pikemen and heavy cavalry supported by war elephants. At first things seemed to go well, but the battles Pyrrhus won were at the price of heavy casualties among his soldiers, coining the term 'pyrrhic victory' for any success bought at too high a price. Despite these disasters the Romans formed another army to continue the struggle and finally won a great victory in 275 BC.

The Romans had faced a professional army under the greatest general alive and emerged victorious. Within the space of a century Rome came to dominate the Mediterranean world, winning two massive struggles with the Carthaginian Empire and then shattering the armies of the great kingdoms of the Hellenistic East. The Greek historian Polybius wrote a detailed history trying to explain how this previously little-regarded Italian city had so suddenly and dramatically burst on to the world stage. For Polybius two factors above all else were fundamental to Rome's success. The first was her well-balanced political constitution which gave her the internal stability that all Greek city states had tended to lack. The second was her fine military system, an institution that we can at last describe with some confidence.

THE ROMAN ARMY IN THE MID REPUBLIC

The basic unit of the Roman army was the legion, which was composed of five elements: cavalry, light infantry and three types of heavy infantry. The most prestigious were the cavalry or *equites*, recruited from the wealthiest citizens able to afford a horse and its trappings. Many young aristocrats began their political career by making a name for themselves in the cavalry. They were equipped with a round shield, helmet and body armour, and armed with a sword and one or several javelins. Roman cavalry were enthusiastic and brave, but better at making a charge on the battlefield than patrolling or scouting. The most serious weakness of the Roman cavalry was that there were not very many of them. Each legion had only three hundred horsemen, divided into ten troops (*turmae*) of thirty each, commanded by three decurions.

These Roman soldiers on the first-century altar of Domitius Ahenobarbus probably give a good indication of the uniform of legionaries in the late third and second centuries BC, for the frieze seems to depict a historical scene. Both wear mail armour, slightly different bronze helmets and carry long, oval shields. The man on the right clearly has a pugio *dagger on his left hip.*

The heavy infantry, like the hoplite phalanx, was composed of all those citizens able to afford the panoply. Unlike the phalanx they fought in three separate lines, membership of which was determined not by wealth but by age and experience. The youngest soldiers or *hastati* formed the front line. Behind them came the *principes*, men in their late twenties or early thirties, the age considered by the Romans to be the prime of life, and in the rear were the older veterans, the *triarii*. All wore a bronze helmet and carried a long, semi-cylindrical body shield, constructed of plywood and covered with calfskin to give it an effective mixture of flexibility and resilience. The wealthier men wore a mail or scale cuirass, but some made do with a simple bronze plate strapped in place over the chest.

All Roman infantrymen were first and foremost swordsmen, and by the last quarter of the third century at the latest, this sword was the famous *gladius hispaniensis* or Spanish sword. With a blade less than 60 centimetres (2 feet) long, the *gladius* was well balanced for both cutting and thrusting, and its manufacture from high-quality steel allowed it to preserve a wickedly sharp edge. The *triarii* carried a long hoplite spear, but the other lines already used the *pilum*, the weapon which, with the *gladius,* was to be the trademark of the Roman legionary. The *pilum* had a wooden shaft of about 120 centimetres (4 feet) in length, which was topped by a 60–90-centimetre (2–3-foot) narrow iron shank leading to a short pyramidal point, which with all the weight of the weapon behind it was designed for maximum armour penetration. The long narrow shank gave it the reach to cause a wound after punching through a shield. The barbed point made it difficult to withdraw from a shield, so that the enemy was forced to drop it. Modern experiments with reconstructed *pila* have suggested a maximum range of about 30 metres (100 feet), but an effective range of about half that. Polybius tells us that each man carried two *pila*, one significantly heavier than the other, but it has proved difficult to categorize the archaeological remains so precisely.

Each of the three lines was divided into ten maniples, those of the *hastati* and *principes* consisting of 120 to 160 men apiece, whereas the less numerous *triarii* formed maniples of sixty men. In battle formation, the *triplex acies*, or maniples, were deployed in a chequerboard or *quincunx*, the units of *principes* covering the gaps between the maniples of *hastati*, while the intervals in their own line were covered by the maniples of the *triarii*. The *triarii* provided the legion's ultimate reserve and spent most of a battle waiting at the rear, kneeling behind their shields, with their spears braced against the ground. They only became involved if the battle was particularly hard fought, and the Roman proverb 'It's down to the *triarii*' was used to describe any desperate situation. The maniple of two centuries was the lowest independent sub-unit of the legion, but each century still carried its own standard, or *signum*, and was led by a centurion. Each centurion was backed up by two subordinates, the *signifer*, or standard-bearer, and the second-in-command, or *optio*, who stood behind the rear rank and kept the men in formation. At least at the beginning of this period centurions were elected by the legions, but appointed their subordinates. The senior centurion stood on the right of the maniple.

The last element of the legion was the light infantry, or *velites*. There were normally 1,200 of these armed with a small round shield, a bundle of light javelins and, at least by the early second century, a *gladius*. They were recruited from the poorer citizens in the state and also those of the higher property qualification who were not yet considered old enough to join the *hastati*. The *velites* do not seem to have been divided into any formal units and fought in support of either the heavy infantry or the cavalry depending on the situation. This gave the Polybian legion a total of 4,200 infantry and 300 cavalry. In times of particular crisis the number of infantry might be increased to 6,000, but this was done without ever varying the number of *triarii*. The sixty centurions and thirty decurions were overseen by six military tribunes, two of whom held overall command of the legion at any one time. The tribunes were elected, usually from young aristocrats in the earliest stages of a political career. A consul was normally given an army of two legions, but in times of crisis this was increased to four. In addition to the Roman legions, each army included a similarly sized contingent of allies. About 4–5,000 infantry and 900 cavalry formed an *ala*, which was commanded by officers known as prefects who were invariably Romans. In battle, a consular army formed with the two *alae* on either side of a centre composed of the Roman legions, so that they were usually referred to as the 'Left' and 'Right' *alae*. A special body of troops, the *extraordinarii*, was detached from these and placed at the immediate disposal of the consul. Often used as shock troops, in an advance these formed the vanguard, while in a retreat they brought up the rear.

Another scene from the Ahenobarbus altar shows a senior officer, most probably a military tribune. He has a muscled cuirass and two rows of fringed pteruges as decoration over his tunic.

The Roman army in this period was a curious mixture of a citizen militia and a professional force. In many ways it had much in common with the conscript armies raised in Europe after the French Revolution. All citizens possessing property above a set level were eligible for service. They served for the duration of a conflict and then returned to civilian life; they were obliged to serve the state in this way for up to sixteen campaigns. While enrolled in the army, citizens were paid and fed by the state and agreed to subject themselves to a very harsh system of discipline, binding themselves at a formal parade by taking the solemn military oath (the *sacramentum*) to obey the consuls. This discipline not only dealt with their behaviour in battle, but regulated every aspect of their service life. Serious crimes, such as neglect of guard duty, theft from comrades or homosexual acts, were punishable by death, with lesser misdemeanours resulting in a flogging. If a whole unit disgraced itself in battle it was liable to decimation, the execution of one man in ten. The survivors lived on in public disgrace, forced to camp outside the defences of the main camp and fed on barley, not wheat. All the many legal defences a Roman citizen possessed against the arbitrary exercise of power by a magistrate in peacetime he lost on entering the army. Many of the institutions of the later professional army already existed by the second century BC at the very latest. The army's discipline was reflected in one of its most famous practices, the construction of a marching camp at the end of each day's march. Polybius describes at great length the procedure for marking out the camp, always built to set dimensions with a uniform plan of roads and tent lines so that it resembled an ordered city. One story claimed that Pyrrhus first realized that he was not facing mere barbarians when he saw a Roman army camped for the night.

The draconian discipline formed only part of the picture. The soldiers were drawn from the same citizen body that elected the army's commanders. There seems to have been a strong sense of shared duty to the state among both the soldiers and their commanders. The ordinary soldiers possessed a freedom to address their commanders which belied the rigid hierarchy but reflected the political life of Rome. Throughout the third century BC there is no evidence for any widespread attempts to avoid military service. Military and civilian life overlapped for all classes. Polybius was full of praise for the encouragement the Romans gave to their brave soldiers. At the end of a campaign, or after a great battle, a parade was held by the army at which the individuals who had displayed conspicuous gallantry were decorated and acclaimed by their comrades. Decorations included ornamental spears or horse trappings, while the first man over the wall of an enemy fortress received a gold wreath, the *corona muralis*. Highest of all was the *corona civica*, the simple laurel crown awarded for saving the life of another citizen. For the rest of their lives these men were allowed to wear their decorations during state festivals, to the admiration of the whole community. For the aristocracy such acclaim was a major asset in a political career.

The strict Roman discipline and the institutions of apparent professionalism should not conceal the fact that Roman armies were impermanent and of very varied quality. The longer an army served, the more efficient it became. Some of the legions enrolled during the Punic wars served for decades and reached the highest state of efficiency. An extreme case was the two legions formed from the survivors of the disaster at Cannae in 216 BC, who served throughout the rest of the conflict and fought with great distinction at Zama in 202. Some of these men were still on active service in Macedonia and awaiting discharge more than twenty years after their original enlisting. Yet once an army was discharged, its accumulated experience disappeared. Individual soldiers were likely to serve in the army again, but they would not do so in the same units. Therefore each time a Roman army was raised, the process of training and disciplining it began afresh. Although each levy included men with prior experience, this facilitated the training process but did not make it unnecessary. A wise commander took great care to prepare his army for battle, training them and gradually giving them confidence by providing minor victories. Hannibal won his greatest victories over Roman armies that were under-prepared for battle. The temporary nature of each Roman army meant that they lacked a cadre of technical experts, the trained professionals who provided the siege engineers in Hellenistic armies. If the Romans failed to take a fortified city by surprise assault or treachery, they were not skilled at prosecuting a formal siege and usually had to rely on starving the enemy into submission.

THE ARMY IN BATTLE

The manipular legion was designed for fighting pitched battles. Its organization allowed it only one formation, the *triplex acies* with the three lines of heavy infantry supporting each other to place maximum pressure on an enemy to the front. When a Roman army was close to the enemy, the legions marched in three parallel columns, the *hastati* on the left, the *principes* in the centre and the *triarii* on the right. To deploy into the battle formation these columns wheeled to the right to form the *triplex acies*. Each maniple had to be positioned carefully in relation to its neighbours in its own and the other two lines to ensure that the legion's front was properly and uniformly supported. Even when the army had camped only a few kilometres from the enemy it still formed itself into three columns and marched to within one and a half kilometres or less of the enemy position, and then, at the point which would form the left of the army's position, wheeled to the right and marched along the army's intended front to form the *triplex acies*. It was a time-consuming process, even in an experienced and well-drilled army, the whole column having to stop and wait as each maniple reached its appointed position and closed up from marching formation into battle formation before it could move forward again. Deploying a Roman army took hours, and required constant supervision from the tribunes. If the enemy threatened then the army's deployment was covered by the cavalry, perhaps supported by some of the *velites* or *extraordinarii*. More often than not the enemy was too busy forming his own battle line to pose much of a threat. Hellenistic and Carthaginian armies used a similar processional system of deployment to the Romans, forming the army into a column with each unit in the order it would take in the battle line. Since they normally massed their infantry in a single deeper line they tended to use a single column rather than the Romans' three, but the process was equally laborious.

The marching camp assisted in this process. As important as the formal and fixed positioning of the tent lines were the spaces between them containing paths and roadways. The army used these and the *intervallum*, the wide-open strip of land separating the tents from the ramparts, to form up into the columns which it used to deploy, the position of the tent lines automatically placing the maniples in the right order. Each of the three columns left via one of the four gates, the cavalry often using the remaining exit. If the army had deployed into battle order but not fought then it was able to retire to the camp in order, each of the three lines of the army, beginning with the *triarii* in the rear, forming a column and marching back to its tents.

The chequerboard formation used by the Roman legions has often been misunderstood and few scholars have been willing to believe that the maniples actually fought with such wide gaps between them. If they had done so then would not a charging enemy, especially a mob of howling Gauls, have swept through the gaps in the line of *hastati*, outflanking each of the maniples and routing them in an instant? It has conventionally been assumed that, while the Romans may have advanced with the maniples in the *quincunx*, they formed an unbroken line before they reached the enemy. Advancing with intervals between an army's units is more obviously intelligible. Even on a perfectly flat parade ground it is very difficult for a unit to march in a perfectly straight line and any unevenness will drastically increase the likelihood of veering to one side or the other. If there are not significant gaps between units advancing on a parallel course then they run the risk of colliding with each other, disordering both and making it difficult for their officers to control them.

None of our ancient sources imply that the *quincunx* was only intended for approaching the enemy, and that the gaps between the maniples were filled just before contact. In fact for the Romans to have halted and changed formation just in front of the enemy would seem a dangerous practice. It is often forgotten that all of Rome's opponents must have had gaps in their own lines to allow these to move. We are told explicitly that at Trebia and Magnesia the Carthaginian and Seleucid light infantry respectively were able to advance past, fight a skirmish in front of, and then retire through the gaps in their own main infantry line. Polybius tells us that Pyrrhus mixed clearly distinct units of his own pikemen and Tarentine infantry in the lines of the main phalanx, while at Cannae Hannibal's front line alternated units of Spanish and Gallic infantry. The size of these units is unclear, but Polybius employs one of the words he also uses for maniple, and which was applied by later authors to the cohort of the Principate. This makes it likely that we are dealing with detachments of several hundred men, and almost certainly less than a thousand. The smallest independent unit in the Hellenistic military manuals was the *syntagma* of 256 men, which possessed its own standard, commander and musician. At Magnesia Antiochus left intervals each holding two elephants between the ten 1,000-strong, 32-rank deep blocks of his phalanx. Our sources do not suggest that the Romans uniquely formed a battle line with intervals in it, but they do imply that the gaps in a Roman line were wider than was normal. One reason why the *quincunx* did not risk disaster was that the maniples of the line behind covered the intervals in front. An enemy passing through the gaps between the *hastati* risked attack from the *principes*. However, the whole system becomes much more intelligible if it is considered in the light of the nature of heavy infantry combat.

Large-scale hand-to-hand combat has not been a common feature of warfare in recent centuries and it is something that is very hard for us to imagine. All too often our mental picture of a clash between sword- and spear-armed lines owes more to cinematic portrayals of spectacular battle scenes in which all the participants rush around fighting frenzied individual duels. In reality, combat seems to have been a lot more tentative. Battles usually lasted for several hours, and the battle of Pydna in 168 BC, which lasted only an hour, was considered an exceptionally brief affair. For much of this time the main lines of heavy infantry were in contact. Hand-to-hand fighting was physically very fatiguing and emotionally stressful. Actual hand-to-hand fighting can only have lasted for very short periods, and the relatively light casualties suffered in this stage of the fighting seem to support this.

Polybius' Roman legionaries advanced noisily, yelling their war cries and banging their weapons against their shields. Most other infantry advanced in a similar fashion, the aim being to intimidate the enemy by looking and sounding threatening. Ideally, this persuaded the enemy that he had no chance of success and put him to flight long before the two lines met. Somewhere within 30 metres of the enemy, the Romans threw their *pila*, and the barrage of heavy missiles inflicted casualties and further reduced the enemy's confidence. The Roman shield had a horizontal hand-grip and it was impossible for a man to use it in combat and at the same time grip a *pilum* in his left hand. Therefore, each Roman legionary must have thrown both of his *pila* before he reached the enemy. The range of these missiles was so short that a man did not have time to throw two *pila* and then draw his sword if he was advancing into combat. This means that either many *pila* were thrown outside effective range, or that the Romans usually slowed their advance or halted within 30 metres of the enemy. Such a pause in the advance is not as implausible as it may at first seem. The aim of the advance was to intimidate the enemy into an early flight. If neither side managed to gain a significant moral advantage over the other, then each may have lost confidence and been reluctant to close immediately with the enemy.

Whether or not there was an initial check, most armies with a cultural tradition of close combat seem normally to have resumed the advance and reached the enemy in the first wave of the battle. In the resulting combat the opposing front ranks hacked, thrust and stabbed at each other, the Romans punching at the enemy with their shield bosses. When an enemy was knocked down or killed there was a chance to step into his place and attempt to fight a way into the enemy formation. More often than not the man attempting this was himself killed, but if a few men managed to work their way into the enemy ranks and break their formation then there was a real chance that the enemy would panic and flee. If neither side achieved this after a few minutes of fighting then the opposing lines drew back. Separated by perhaps as little as a few metres, the two lines then jeered and glared at each other, throwing any remaining missiles, as each attempted to build up enough energy and confidence to step forward and renew the struggle. The longer the battle went on the harder it became each time to persuade the line to close once more. Officers played a vital role in urging on their men to sustain this effort. Centurions were elected from those with a record for gallantry and the Romans took great care to praise and reward the soldiers who displayed individual boldness. Compulsion and fear of punishment also had a part to play in giving a unit the stamina to stay close to the enemy. The men in the front rank, the ones who actually fought and were in greatest danger, had to stay there as long as those in the ranks behind stayed in position, since the latter's physical presence made escape impossible. A deeper formation gave a unit greater staying power in combat by making it hard for most of the men to flee. So did the presence of *optiones*, the centurions' senior subordinates, behind the rear rank, physically pushing the men back into place. The longer a unit was close to the enemy the more its formation and cohesion dissolved. Men increasingly followed their instincts, the bravest pushing to the front, the most timid trying to slip away to the rear, while the majority remained somewhere in the middle. At any time they might follow the example of the timid and the unit dissolve into rout, and this possibility became greater the longer a unit did not advance or seem to be making progress. Most casualties on an ancient battlefield occurred when a unit fled from combat. The ones who died first were those who were slowest in turning to flee, so the men in the centre of a formation, able to see little of what was going on, were always on the verge of nervous panic.

Most armies deployed with a single main line, which as a result tended to be deep and have great staying power in combat. In the Roman *triplex acies* more than half of the infantry were kept in reserve and were not involved in the initial combat. Instead, the rear two lines advanced in turn to join the existing combat at later stages of the battle. Ideally, the *hastati* fought the main enemy line to a standstill, their discipline and the leadership of their centurions keeping them in contact with the enemy, who was probably more numerous and in a deeper formation. Then the *principes* advanced into the combat zone, their freshness and enthusiasm urging the whole Roman line to advance with a confidence which the enemy by that time might not be able to match. The skill of a Roman commander lay in committing his second and third lines at the right time. If it was left too long then the *hastati* might buckle under enemy pressure. Too soon and the value of adding a fresh contingent of troops to a combat might be lost. It was exceptionally rare for the Romans to withdraw an entire line and replace it with one from behind. Usually the troops in the rear lines were fed into the combat to support the troops already engaged.

In this context the *triplex acies* offered a more effective use of an army's numbers. The intervals between maniples were necessary to allow fresh troops to join the struggle. When combat between lines was so tentative there was little danger that an enemy would stream through the gaps and swamp the whole line. At Pydna the Macedonian phalanx advanced too far and too fast and began to break up into its constituent units. Eventually the Romans were able to exploit this, individual centurions leading parties of men to infiltrate the phalanx and attack the helpless pikemen from the flanks. This only happened after the two sides had charged each other and fought a long hand-to-hand combat. Even then it only happened through the bold leadership of individuals. The ancient battlefield was a far more open place than is often imagined.

THE FIRST PUNIC WAR AND NAVAL WARFARE

Carthage was the great mercantile empire of the western Mediterranean. Originally a Phoenician colony, its language, culture and religion remained essentially Semitic, but it had long been on the fringes of the Greek world. Greek political theorists admired its balanced constitution, which gave it the internal political stability which most city states lacked. By the third century BC Carthage dominated most of North Africa and a large part of the southern coastline of Spain. Like most city states, Carthage was jealous of the rights granted to its citizens and had not extended these to the vast majority of the subject and allied peoples in her territories. Carthaginian citizens were few in number and only obliged to perform military service in the face of a threat to the city itself. Therefore Carthage relied on hiring armies of mercenaries whenever it needed to fight a war on land. The city's wealth was based on maritime trade and the greatest permanent expense was the maintenance of the vast fleet created to protect this. Ships were mass produced in their hundreds; archaeological excavation of the site of a wrecked Punic galley revealed that its timbers had been shaped and numbered before construction, each piece presumably being produced to a standard plan. This great fleet was housed in the huge artificial harbour constructed in Carthage itself and other smaller ports throughout Carthage's territories. Its crews were paid and many of the city's poorest citizens received a steady income from regular service in the fleet. One of the reasons for Carthage's political stability was that its poorer elements were provided with a livelihood in this way.

The First Punic War began when both Rome and Carthage answered a call for assistance from different factions within the same Sicilian community. Throughout the resulting twenty-three-year conflict the fighting was to focus overwhelmingly on Sicily as each side attacked the other's allies and strongholds on the island. Although there was much land fighting, this was overwhelmingly a naval war, and all the decisive moves occurred at sea. Rome's first military expedition outside the Italian

The Punic Wars

The Punic Wars were fought on a larger scale than almost any other conflicts of Classical Antiquity. The First Punic War (265–241 BC) began accidentally. It was primarily a naval war, with each side employing fleets of hundreds of quinqueremes. Although the navy had been created almost from nothing during the war, it proved highly effective, winning all but one of the major battles, and its main losses were caused by the weather.

The Second Punic War (218–202 BC) was caused by the Carthaginians' dissatisfaction with the Peace Treaty of 241 BC and Rome's overbearing attitude.

The Third Punic War (149–146 BC) developed from Roman fears that Carthage was once again becoming a strong power. It ended in the total destruction of the Carthaginian State.

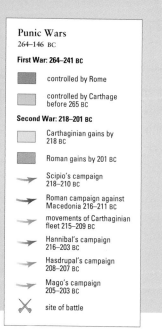

Punic Wars
264–146 BC

First War: 264–241 BC

controlled by Rome

controlled by Carthage before 265 BC

Second War: 218–201 BC

Carthaginian gains by 218 BC

Roman gains by 201 BC

Scipio's campaign 218–210 BC

Roman campaign against Macedonia 216–211 BC

movements of Carthaginian fleet 215–209 BC

Hannibal's campaign 216–203 BC

Hasdrubal's campaign 208–207 BC

Mago's campaign 205–203 BC

site of battle

ATLANTIC OCEAN

Numantia

Douro

CELTIBERIANS

Hispania

LUSITANIANS

Tagus

Guadiana

Saguntum

Onoba

Guadalquivir

Ilipa 206

Baecula

IBERIANS

Carthago N. 209

Malaca

Car

Rusaddir

Mulucha

N

A

0   200 km

0   200 miles

peninsula was also to be her first large-scale experience of war at sea.

The great naval battles of Greek history had been fought principally by triremes, galleys with three banks of oars with a single rower to each oar. By the third century the trireme (a 'three') had been outclassed by the quinquereme (a 'five'), but the precise nature of this ship remains obscure. Clearly it had something, probably rowers, at a ratio of five to three compared to the trireme, but it is not clear how these were

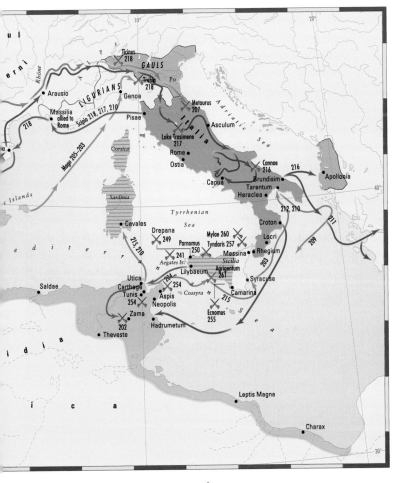

deployed. There were two basic tactical options for all sizes of ancient warships. Either they attempted to grapple with an enemy ship and board it, relying on the crew's numbers or fighting quality to capture the ship in mêlée, or they tried to ram the enemy and pierce his hull or shear off his oars. Although galleys were usually fitted with a mast and sail, the wind was too uncertain an agent of motion to allow them to fight when they did not possess missile weapons capable of inflicting serious harm on the enemy. Mobility depended on a ship's rowers, and galleys were effectively constructed around these. In proportion to their size, galleys carried far larger crews than later sailing ships and nearly all of these men were rowers. Space was highly limited, especially so on a quinquereme which, despite their 40 per cent increase in crew, do not seem to have been much larger than triremes. The weight of the rowers provided much of a galley's ballast, making it unwise for any great number of them to leave their seats at the same time. There was also very little space available on a ship to carry provisions of food and

The reconstruction of the trireme ('three') and its sea trials greatly increased our understanding of ancient warships. The trireme proved capable of making 8 knots in short bursts and could maintain a steady 4 knots for hours on end. Under sail it also reached speeds of 8 knots, but wind power was too uncertain to be used in battle, since ancient warships needed to manoeuvre quickly.

water. The result was that not only was travel by sea uncomfortable, but very long, continuous journeys were simply impossible. A voyage of more than a few days between friendly ports was risky. If possible the galley was beached each night and the crew allowed to rest, but this was only practical when the shore was not hostile. Most naval battles throughout history have tended to occur relatively close to the shore, largely as a result of the real difficulty fleets had in locating each other in the vast expanse of ocean. In the ancient world this was an absolute necessity, simply because the fleets could not risk moving too far from the shore. Sicily provided the ideal theatre for a naval conflict because its numerous anchorages were within practical range of the fleets operating from home bases in Italy and North Africa.

Geography and the might of the Carthaginian navy meant that the conflict was likely to be dominated by sea-power, but at the beginning of the war Rome was not a naval power, largely because she had never needed to be in the past. She may have possessed a small number of ships, and some of her Italian allies certainly had their own navies, but they could not have hoped to form a serious rival to the Punic fleet, especially since it is possible that no state in Italy at that time possessed any quinqueremes. When in 261–260 BC the Romans decided to build a hundred quinqueremes, Polybius claims that they copied the design of a Carthaginian ship which had run aground and been captured earlier in the war. The story is one example of the pride the Romans took in their ability to copy the best weapons and tactics of their enemies, but may still be genuine. Polybius states that they trained the ships' crews while the fleet was under construction, building tiered benches on land to practise rowing. Yet even with this training, the new Roman fleet lacked the experience and skill of the well-drilled Carthaginian crews and the naval war did not start well for the Romans. The fleet's commander was surprised in harbour and all the seventeen ships with him were captured by a Punic squadron.

The tactics of ramming required skilful handling of a ship and the Romans may have realized that they could not match their opponents in this, as from the beginning of the war they were to rely on boarding the enemy. With this in mind they designed the 'Crow' (*corvus*), a boarding ramp fitted with a spike which stuck fast in an opponent's deck, locking the two ships together. Once grappled in this way no amount of skill on the part of the Carthaginian crew could break their ship free and the Roman legionaries swarmed across the bridge and settled the affair with their ferocity in hand-to-hand combat. The new device was tested when the massed fleets clashed off Mylae in north-eastern Sicily, 130 Carthaginian ships facing a slightly smaller number of Roman ones. The Carthaginian admiral, commanding the fleet in a ship that had once belonged to Pyrrhus, was confident in his crews' superiority and attacked aggressively. The Carthaginians did not realize the purpose of the *corvi* until they began to drop, the beaks spearing into their decks and grappling them fast. Thirty ships, including the flagship, were captured by the Roman infantry, who flooded over the ramps. Attempts to swing round and outflank the Romans were foiled when the Romans turned to face or swung their *corvi* round to drop over either side of the ship. The battle was a total success for the Romans with between thirty and fifty ships captured by the end of the day. The prows (*rostrata*) of these prizes were cut off and sent to decorate the Speaker's platform in Rome, which in time gave it a new name.

In 256 BC the Romans repeated their success at the battle of Ecnomus, at which each side probably mustered well over 200 ships (Polybius gives the Carthaginian strength as 350 and the Roman as 330 which, if correct, would make this one of the largest naval battles in history). The Carthaginians had found no counter to the *corvi*, but in the next years few years the weather dealt Rome a series of severe blows when three fleets were wrecked in storms. Hundreds of ships were lost and the drowned numbered tens of thousands. Poor Roman seamanship may have been to blame, but it is also possible that the *corvi*'s weight made the ships less seaworthy. Then at Drepana in 249 BC the Romans suffered their only defeat in a fleet action, a disaster blamed on impiety when the consul, Publius Claudius Pulcher, ignored the unfavourable auspices. When the chickens refused to eat (and by so doing signify divine favour), he is said to have hurled them over the side, proclaiming that if they would not eat, then they would drink. These Roman disasters and Carthaginian exhaustion brought a lull, but in 242 BC the war was decided at sea when the Romans, having risked the creation of another fleet, smashed the last Punic fleet near the Aegates Islands. In the resulting peace treaty Carthage gave up both her fleet and all her possessions in Sicily.

LAND WARFARE AGAINST CARTHAGE
AND THE HELLENISTIC WORLD

Rome's army was still essentially a citizen militia, but all the great powers of the Mediterranean world relied almost entirely on professional soldiers. In the case of Carthage these were mercenaries hired in contingents from Africa and Europe, so that Punic armies were usually a polyglot of nationalities. Hannibal's army included units of spearmen fighting in a phalanx and heavy cavalry from Libya, wild Numidian light cavalry riding bareback, and horse and foot from the tribes of Spain. To these he later added Gallic warriors from northern Italy and troops such as Bruttians, Campanians and Samnites from Rome's disaffected allies. Such armies were difficult to control, but the longer they served together under the same Carthaginian officers the more efficient they became. The nucleus of Hannibal's army were the troops that had fought a series of hard campaigns in Spain under his own and his father's command, and this long experience, combined with his genius and the skill of his officers, turned them into the highly efficient army he took into Italy. This was a force capable of such difficult operations as the night march that secretly put them into ambush positions at Lake Trasimene in 217 BC. Each Carthaginian army was a separate entity that built up a command structure around, and owed loyalty to, a particular commander, or sometimes his family. Each national contingent may have understood the relationship in a different way, perhaps owing loyalty to a great warrior who rewarded them or simply to the paymaster who provided for them. Armies raised at different times under different leaders did not co-operate well, and it has been pointed out that each of the three lines deployed by Hannibal at Zama was formed by troops raised separately. The first line consisted of troops originally raised by Hannibal's brother Mago, the second of contingents raised in Africa for the defence of Carthage, and the third was composed of the veterans of the Italian campaign. While Hannibal spoke to his veterans in person, he ordered their own officers to speak to the other two lines. In the battle itself the first and second lines did not co-operate well, Polybius even claiming that fighting broke out between them at one stage.

The armies raised by Macedon and the Seleucid Empire were far more homogenous, being recruited primarily from Macedonian citizens or their descendants, settled

HANNIBAL'S CAMPAIGNS IN ITALY

The march of Hannibal's army from Spain to Italy in 218 BC was one of the epics of ancient history. Between 218–216 BC Hannibal won an unbroken series of victories at Ticinus, Trebia, Trasimene, and Cannae. Somehow the Romans absorbed their appalling losses and continued the war, when any other contemporary state would have accepted peace terms at this point. After Cannae, much of southern Italy defected to Hannibal, who was forced to fight to protect his new allies. Although never able to defeat Hannibal in battle, the Romans gradually used their superior numbers to defeat his allies. In 207 BC Hannibal's brother brought a fresh army to Italy, but it was a sign of the experience the Romans had gained since 218 BC that it was rapidly cornered by a superior force and destroyed. In 203 BC Hannibal was finally recalled to defend Carthage from the Roman invaders and led his unbeaten army from Italy. The next year he suffered his only defeat in a pitched battle at Zama, bringing the war to an end.

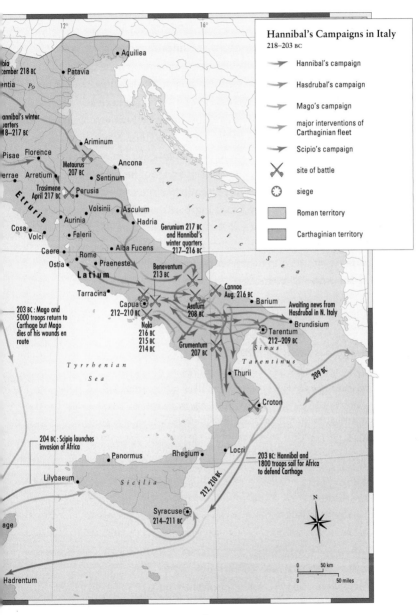

Hannibal's Campaigns in Italy
218–203 BC

Hannibal's campaign

Hasdrubal's campaign

Mago's campaign

major interventions of
Carthaginian fleet

Scipio's campaign

site of battle

siege

Roman territory

Carthaginian territory

throughout the conquests of Alexander the Great. The king still fought at the head of his aristocratic cavalry as Philip and Alexander had done, sharing the dangers with his army and so justifying his place in society in the best warrior tradition. The men were well-trained, disciplined professionals organized into units with a clearly defined command structure controlled by officers with good technical knowledge of soldiering. Hellenistic armies were in many ways more efficient than Roman armies, but they were also more fragile. Trained soldiers were difficult to replace from the limited resources available to each kingdom, and very high losses to the army might not be made good for a generation. Although Carthage usually had the resources to hire more mercenaries, it took a long time to give these the cohesion necessary to create an effective army. The Romans were unique among ancient states in maintaining the principle of a citizen militia, but turning it into a force capable of standing up to a modern, professional army. Roman citizens accepted the burden of a harsh military discipline and service, in many cases for the duration of a war, during which time they were trained to a high level of efficiency. Polybius claimed that the total number of Roman citizens and allies liable to military service at the outbreak of the Second Punic War was more than 700,000. Even if this claimed total is too large, the real figure was certainly considerable and allowed Rome to endure the appalling casualties inflicted on her by Hannibal and still raise more legions, as she had been able to cope with the equally terrible losses suffered at sea during the First Punic War. No other contemporary state could have weathered such disasters and still gone on to win the conflict.

The art of war in the third century had largely been created in the endemic warfare between the kingdoms created when Alexander's empire fragmented. These conflicts were fought between very similar professional armies which were highly skilled but could not afford heavy casualties. The objective was to gain victory at minimum cost and even heavy losses to the opposition were to be avoided since it was better to capture enemy soldiers and recruit them than to kill them. A war was won when the enemy could be persuaded that he had nothing to gain from fighting on, and so was willing to come to terms. Most conflicts were ended by negotiation once one side had gained a clear advantage. A complex system evolved in which quite minor details such as the amount paid to ransom prisoners clearly indicated which side had been victorious and by how great a margin. More seriously, losing a war usually meant giving up territory and perhaps paying an indemnity, but wars were fought to weaken, not destroy, the enemy and a struggle to the death would have been in no one's interest. An enemy was persuaded to concede defeat by putting pressure on him by raiding his fields or capturing his cities, but, more than anything else, a victory in a pitched battle was the best way to win a war. Professional armies were as much intended for fighting big battles as the hoplite phalanx had been, being merely more sophisticated in their approach. The theoretical literature on the skills of generalship which began to be written at this time was overwhelmingly concerned with how and when to fight a battle. Strategy as it would be understood today played little part in the wars of this period. Generals manoeuvred to create the most favourable opportunity to defeat the enemy field army. A battle was to be sought whenever a commander was confident that he would win, and needed no higher purpose.

Battles fought between armies produced by the same military doctrines were uncertain affairs, and an indecisive result with heavy casualties on each side was useless and damaging to both parties. These conditions produced a very tentative style of fighting. Armies tended to move rapidly to confront each other, since defeating the enemy army was their main function, but then became very cautious, camping only a few kilometres apart for days or even weeks without fighting. Often each side marched out and deployed in battle formation every day, the two lines within a few hundred metres of each other, yet neither was willing to advance the final short distance and force a battle. Frequent skirmishes and single combats were fought between detachments of cavalry and light infantry, and victories in these helped to develop a feeling of superiority over the enemy. The general's task was to raise his army to the highest pitch of confidence before exposing it to battle. Military manuals encouraged a commander to seek every advantage, however slight, ranging from ensuring that his army fought with full stomachs against an enemy who was hungry, or that the opposition fought with the sun in their eyes. Such factors did not in themselves determine the outcome of a battle, but each additional advantage gave an army another 'edge' over the opposition. There were times during the latter stages of the First Punic War in Sicily when the rival armies watched each other for months on end, only moving their positions when they ran out of food. Professional armies, unlike hoplites, did not have to return to gather the harvest, so there was no limit to the time spent manoeuvring if neither side saw the chance of a favourable battle.

The Romans had turned their citizen militia into a force capable of facing professional armies, but Polybius still saw them as rather old-fashioned in their straightforward and open approach to warfare. They expected battles to be almost as simple as the old hoplite clashes, and showed a willingness to fight immediately even if the conditions were not ideal. Both Pyrrhus and Hannibal outclassed the first Roman commanders sent against them and brought them to battle at the time and place of their own choosing. Hannibal's great victories of 218–216 BC were fought on open ground which favoured his numerically superior cavalry and exploited the varying attributes of his infantry contingents with great skill, especially at Cannae. One reason for the poor showing of Roman commanders was that they found themselves in charge of far larger armies than most would have experienced previously. To confront Hannibal the two consuls combined their armies, mustering four legions in 218 BC and a massive total of eight in 216 BC. It had been very rare for both consuls to unite their forces in the past and this was reflected in the *ad hoc* command structure adopted whereby the two men commanded on alternate days. This, combined with the great numbers of troops involved, tended to make their movements erratic and rather clumsy. Polybius represents

The dusty plain of Cannae today is peaceful and it is hard to imagine the carnage of 2 August 216 BC when over 50,000 men were killed in only a few square miles. The white buildings on the horizon mark the most probable location for Hannibal's camp. In the middle distance, the line of trees marks the modern line of the River Aufidius, but its course in 216 BC is unknown.

Hannibal's victories as greatly eased by this divided command which produced fiercely divided councils, although maybe these passages are influenced by his desire to exonerate the ancestors of his patron Scipio Aemilianus from responsibility for these disasters. Although often outmanoeuvred by more skilful opponents, Roman armies were still tough opponents who continued fighting long after most other armies would have conceded defeat. In part this was a result of the harsh military discipline which inflicted severe penalties on soldiers who fled even from the most desperate situation. The survivors of Cannae were formed into two legions that were exiled from Italy and sent to fight for the duration of the war in Sicily and Africa. The Roman *triplex acies* contributed to the resilience of Roman legions even in defeat, giving their formation depth and providing reserve troops throughout the line. Although far lower than the massive casualties Hannibal inflicted on the armies he destroyed at Trebia, Trasimene and Cannae, his own men suffered heavily as the Romans fought to the last. The casualties Pyrrhus suffered in defeating the Romans became proverbial.

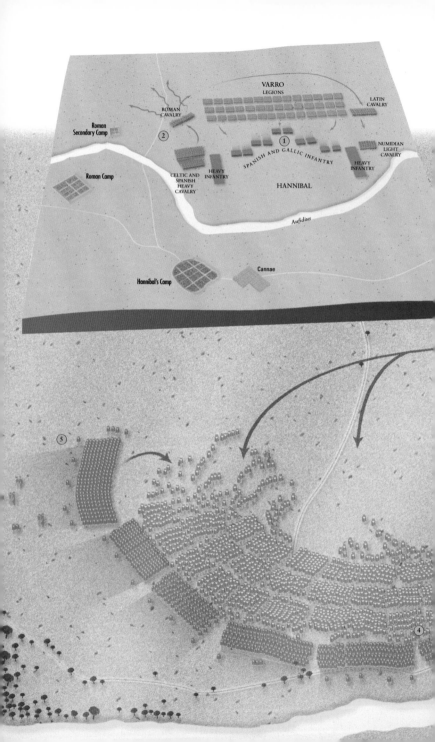

VARRO
LEGIONS

LATIN
CAVALRY

ROMAN
CAVALRY

Roman
Secondary Camp

②

①

SPANISH AND GALLIC INFANTRY

NUMIDIAN
LIGHT
CAVALRY

CELTIC AND
SPANISH
HEAVY
CAVALRY

HEAVY
INFANTRY

HEAVY
INFANTRY

Roman Camp

HANNIBAL

Aufidius

Cannae

Hannibal's Camp

⑤

④

CANNAE

Hannibal's victory at Cannae was his greatest achievement. In an open plain he encircled and destroyed a numerically superior Roman army, killing nearly 50,000 men and capturing around 20,000 more for the loss of 5,700 of his own men. It is now uncertain on which bank of the River Aufidius the battle was fought. This map shows the modern course of the river.

1. Hannibal advances the centre of his line toward the Romans, while his flanks stand fast

2. The Carthaginian heavy cavalry attack the Roman cavalry, driving them from the battlefield. They then cross the rear of the Roman army and attack the rear of the Latin left flank cavalry, who are already engaged by Hannibal's Numidian light cavalry

3. The remaining Roman cavalry are driven from the field

4. The Carthaginian centre comes under intense pressure from the Legions and is forced back. Hannibal encourages them in person and puts up a hard fight before they withdraw. The Romans surge into the gap finally created in the Punic line, reserve maniples being committed to support the apparent success

5. The Roman formation loses its order as a crowd of men packs forward into the enemy centre. Maniples merge into one huge crowd. Hannibal now orders his African infantry to turn inwards and advance against the Roman flanks

6. At this moment the Carthaginian cavalry return and attack the exposed rear of the Roman army

Aufidius

Realizing that no Roman army was yet capable of defeating Hannibal in battle, one Roman commander, Quintus Fabius Maximus, inaugurated a policy of avoiding battle altogether, earning himself the nickname 'the Delayer' (*cunctator*). The Roman army shadowed the movements of Hannibal's army, which was unable to feed itself by foraging off the land if it did not keep moving, observing it and harassing isolated detachments, but never risking a battle in anything save the most favourable circumstances. The fields of the Romans and their allies were raided, cities taken by surprise and some of Rome's allies defected to the enemy, but Hannibal failed in over a decade of operations to inflict so much damage that the Romans were forced to admit defeat. Fabius' policy was logical, fully in keeping with the military science of the period and ultimately successful, but it was unpopular with the Romans, and more than one of his subordinates rejected caution and attacked Hannibal, only to receive a severe handling. The Roman instinct was still for immediate open confrontation with the enemy, and this did produce some great successes against other Carthaginian commanders and the Italian states and Gallic tribes which had defected to Hannibal. As the war progressed the Roman army and its commanders became more and more experienced. The greatest of this new generation of commanders was Publius Cornelius Scipio, who would earn himself the name Africanus. Commanding the Roman army in Spain from 209 BC onwards, Scipio displayed all the skills of an army commander in the Hellenistic tradition, utterly outmanoeuvring his Carthaginian opponent at Ilipa, before going on to lead the Roman invasion of Africa, which brought about the recall of Hannibal from Italy and his first and final defeat in a pitched battle at Zama in 202 BC.

Rome's involvement in the Hellenistic world led directly on from the Second Punic War. Philip V of Macedon had allied himself with Carthage during Rome's darkest hour when Hannibal was rampaging through Italy, and the Romans were quick to remember this after Carthage's defeat, declaring war in 200 BC, despite initial popular resistance to starting another war so soon. Rome had fielded massive armies in the struggle with Carthage, but most of these were demobilized and the armies which fought in the east reverted to the traditional size of two legions plus two allied *alae* under the command of a consul. These armies were conventional in size, but not in the men who composed them. All had served through the bitter struggle with Carthage, serving far more years against tougher opposition than any earlier generation of Romans. These armies, along with those of Scipio in the later years of the Punic War, were the best ever produced by the Republican city militia. Officers and men all knew their job through long experience. The heavy casualties of the war with Hannibal had resulted in the Senate being replenished by men chosen because of conspicuous military service, lowering the age but increasing the experience of the body which provided the army's senior officers. Roman armies of the early second century BC were as well trained and disciplined, and at least as efficient as any of the professional armies they faced. Their tactical system was, however, very different. Hellenistic armies were based around the heavy infantry of the phalanx. The phalanx was no longer composed of hoplites but of pikemen, men wielding the two-handed *sarissa* spear, which sometimes reached a length of 6.4 metres (21 feet). Phalanxes formed at least eight ranks deep, and often deeper, the Seleucids at Magnesia in 190 BC deploying in thirty-two ranks. Such depth gave the phalanx tremendous staying power in combat, and the hedge of spearpoints, five of which projected in front of each man in the first rank, made it very difficult for an enemy to fight his way in from the front. The long pikes themselves also tended to keep the ranks in place and make such a phalanx less subject to the degeneration of cohesion and formation to which most units were subject in combat. A phalanx was very hard for the enemy to break, but it was more likely to win a mêlée by its staying power than its actual fighting qualities. It was also difficult for it to move over anything but the flattest terrain without losing its order. In Alexander's army the phalanx had only ever been intended to pin the enemy and subject him

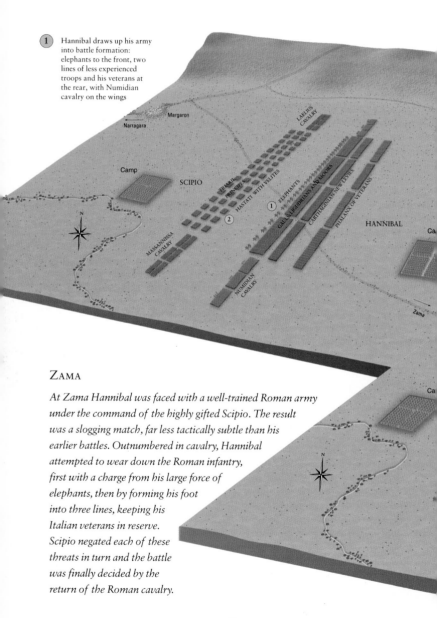

1 Hannibal draws up his army into battle formation: elephants to the front, two lines of less experienced troops and his veterans at the rear, with Numidian cavalry on the wings

Margaron

Narragara

LAELIUS CAVALRY

Camp

SCIPIO

TRIARII

PRINCIPES

HASTATI WITH VELITES

ELEPHANTS

GAULS, LIGURIANS AND MOORS

CARTHAGINIANS & LEVIES

PHALANX OF VETERANS

1

2

HANNIBAL

Ca

MASSANNISSA CAVALRY

NUMIDIAN CAVALRY

Zama

ZAMA

At Zama Hannibal was faced with a well-trained Roman army under the command of the highly gifted Scipio. The result was a slogging match, far less tactically subtle than his earlier battles. Outnumbered in cavalry, Hannibal attempted to wear down the Roman infantry, first with a charge from his large force of elephants, then by forming his foot into three lines, keeping his Italian veterans in reserve. Scipio negated each of these threats in turn and the battle was finally decided by the return of the Roman cavalry.

Ca

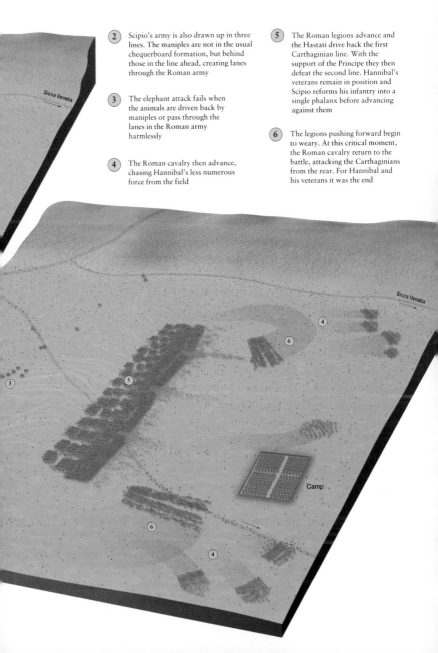

2 Scipio's army is also drawn up in three lines. The maniples are not in the usual chequerboard formation, but behind those in the line ahead, creating lanes through the Roman army

3 The elephant attack fails when the animals are driven back by maniples or pass through the lanes in the Roman army harmlessly

4 The Roman cavalry then advance, chasing Hannibal's less numerous force from the field

5 The Roman legions advance and the Hastati drive back the first Carthaginian line. With the support of the Principe they then defeat the second line. Hannibal's veterans remain in position and Scipio reforms his infantry into a single phalanx before advancing against them

6 The legions pushing forward begin to weary. At this critical moment, the Roman cavalry return to the battle, attacking the Carthaginians from the rear. For Hannibal and his veterans it was the end

Sicca Venetia

Sicca Venetia

Camp

to a steady pressure, the decisive charge being always delivered by the cavalry. By the early second century Hellenistic armies were not capable of fielding the numbers of cavalry seen in the armies of Philip II and Alexander; good horses, just as much as citizen manpower, were always in short supply. As a result they had come to rely more and more on the phalanx to win the battle, a task for which it had never really been suited. To supplement it, and gain an edge in wars often fought against nearly identical armies, various monarchs experimented with gimmick weapons such as scythed chariots and war elephants. The chariots were rarely effective while the elephants, which did win some spectacular successes, were very much a two-edged sword, being inclined to panic and trample both armies indiscriminately.

Hellenistic armies formed with virtually all their units in a single line, centred around the deepest possible infantry phalanx. They were commanded by a king whose role it was to charge at the head of his cavalry in the manner of Alexander. A commander fighting in this way could not have hoped to control troops kept in reserve, since he would have been able to see only what was happening and influence the troops immediately around him. The aim of a commander was to deploy his army in such a way as to put steady pressure on the whole enemy line, before leading in person an irresistible hammer blow at a single point. The Roman system of deploying the legions in three lines ensured that much of the army was kept in reserve. At both Cynoscephalae in 197 BC and Magnesia in 190 BC the Roman line was broken at one point, but the situation was restored by fresh troops from the rear lines. Interestingly, in both cases the reserves were brought up by a relatively junior Roman officer acting on his own initiative, an indication of the high quality of the Roman officer corps at this period. Once the Romans created a breakthrough in the enemy line reserve troops were available to exploit the gap, but their Hellenistic opponents lacked both the reserve troops and the command structure to control them. The manipular legion was flexible while the phalanx was not, and this proved the decisive factor in a clash between the two, especially at Cynoscephalae and Pydna, both of which occurred accidentally and were disorganized affairs.

Another distinction between the two armies was that, while the Romans had adopted the organization and discipline of a 'modern', civilized army, they still fought with great savagery. Alexander's men had been as ferocious as this in their campaigns against the Persians, but the conflicts between the culturally and militarily similar armies of his Successors had made Hellenistic warfare rather more genteel. At Cynoscephalae the defeated Macedonian pikemen stood holding their pikes upright to signify their surrender, but were cut down by the legionaries. Only after someone had explained what the gesture meant to the Roman commander was he able, with some difficulty, to end the massacre.

The Romans fought to destroy the enemy army and end its capacity ever to fight them again. It was a very different culture to the Hellenistic expectation that wars should be ended by negotiation, to avoid unnecessary bloodshed on both sides. Both Pyrrhus and Hannibal made several attempts to open peace negotiations with the Romans after they had defeated them in battle and were surprised at the Romans' refusal to consider a treaty. The Macedonian and Seleucid kings similarly sent their heralds to the Romans on numerous occasions, hoping to end conflict through diplomacy. The Roman negotiating position was always the same: a demand for the other side to concede total defeat regardless of the current military situation. For the Romans war was a life or death struggle which could only end in one of two ways. The first was for the enemy to cease to be a threat, either because it had become a subordinate ally of Rome, or because it had ceased to exist as a political entity. The only alternative was for Rome herself to be destroyed, but this was something that neither Carthage nor any other state possessed the resources to achieve. Not only that, but it is unlikely that any commander produced by the Hellenistic tradition would ever have considered this as an option.

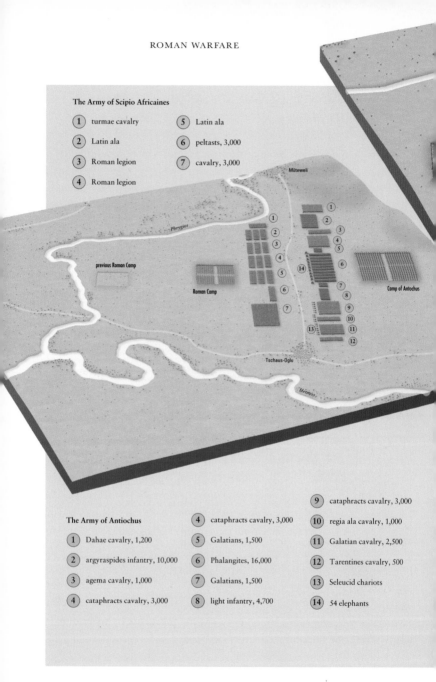

The Army of Scipio Africaines

1. turmae cavalry
2. Latin ala
3. Roman legion
4. Roman legion
5. Latin ala
6. peltasts, 3,000
7. cavalry, 3,000

The Army of Antiochus

1. Dahae cavalry, 1,200
2. argyraspides infantry, 10,000
3. agema cavalry, 1,000
4. cataphracts cavalry, 3,000
4. cataphracts cavalry, 3,000
5. Galatians, 1,500
6. Phalangites, 16,000
7. Galatians, 1,500
8. light infantry, 4,700
9. cataphracts cavalry, 3,000
10. regia ala cavalry, 1,000
11. Galatian cavalry, 2,500
12. Tarentines cavalry, 500
13. Seleucid chariots
14. 54 elephants

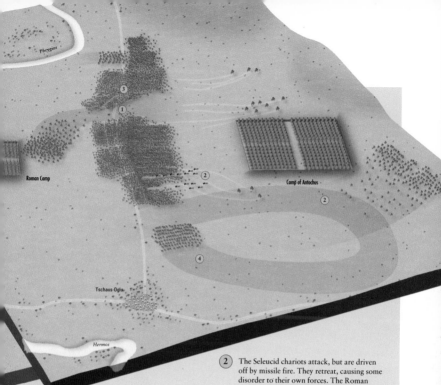

2 The Seleucid chariots attack, but are driven off by missile fire. They retreat, causing some disorder to their own forces. The Roman cavalry advance and drive the Syrian cavalry to the rear

1 Antiochus attacks with agema and cataphracts and breaks through the Roman legion. He leads the cavalry on to the Roman camp, but is checked by the Roman guards left outside the camp. A tribune, Lepidus, manages to reform enough of the routed legion to drive him back

3 The Roman infantry closes with the phalanx and its supporting elephants, driving back the Seleucid skirmishes. Although under pressure, the phalanx stands firm

4 However, confusion is caused in the phalanx when some of the elephants panic and when the Roman cavalry return and attack its flanks and rear. This, combined with the pressure from the legions, is too much and Antiochus's centre dissolves into rout

MAGNESIA

The battle of Magnesia was fought after nearly two weeks of cautious manoeuvring as the rival armies attempted to gain an advantage. The Romans gradually camped further and further forward and deployed their battle line so close to the Seleucids that Antiochus the Great was forced to fight. The Roman armies which fought against the Hellenistic kingdoms in the early second century were exceptionally experienced, well trained and led by men who had learned their trade in the hard school of the war with Hannibal.

The Roman city of Carthage was built on top of the Punic city destroyed in 146 BC,
so that very few remains of the latter are visible today. A few sections of Punic
Carthage have been uncovered by archaeologists and attest to the wealth of the city,
particularly in the period immediately before the final war with Rome.

By his own understanding of war Hannibal won the Second Punic War at Cannae, but the Romans were following a different set of rules and when they did not admit defeat there was little more that he could do to force them. The Romans did not fight for the limited gains other states expected from victory. A defeated enemy was turned into an ally who not only presented no threat to Rome, but actively supported her wars elsewhere. The army they sent against Philip V in 200 was fed by grain supplied by the recently defeated Carthage, and Philip in turn aided the Roman force which fought against the Seleucids. Rome did not tolerate a former enemy existing as anything more than a clearly subordinate ally. The kingdom of Macedonia was dismembered in 168 and Carthage destroyed in 146 BC simply because they had begun to show signs of renewed independence and again assumed the role of potential enemies.

Why did the Romans adopt such an uncompromising attitude to warfare? Their great resources of military manpower, which allowed them to endure the appalling losses of the Punic wars, explains to a great extent how they were able to maintain their resolve. Rome's internal political stability and the strength of the confederation of allies she created around herself were also vital factors. The disaster at the Caudine Forks in 321 BC was the last time that Rome accepted peace as the clear loser in a war. The fourth-century BC struggle against the expanding hill peoples of Central Italy was certainly bitter and may have encouraged the Romans to think of war as a struggle for their very existence. Both Pyrrhus and Hannibal, with their armies marching through Italy, equally seemed to threaten Rome itself, and one of the reasons for the aggressive policy against Macedonia and the Seleucids was the fear that their powerful navies gave them the potential to land an army on the Italian peninsula. Whatever the reasons for it, Rome's attitude to warfare was a major factor in her success in this period and throughout the rest of her history. When wars were decided as soon as one side admitted defeat, it was very difficult for any state to beat a people who were never willing to concede this.

CHAPTER THREE

World Conquest
202 BC–AD 14

Two legionaries depicted on a first-century AD relief from the principia or headquarters building in the fortress at Mainz. The man on the right stands in the classic fighting posture of the Roman soldier, crouching to gain as much protection as possible from his scutum, ready to deliver an underarm thrust from his short sword. The men wear a version of the Imperial Gallic helmet, but it is not clear whether any body armour is shown.

World Conquest 202 BC – AD 14

POLYBIUS CLAIMS THAT Scipio Africanus told his troops before the battle of Zama that they were fighting not just to defeat Carthage, but for the domination of the world. In Polybius' own lifetime Rome had become the greatest power in the Mediterranean. A century and a half later, when the great period of expansion ended with the death of Augustus, the Empire's frontiers lay on the Atlantic coast, the Rhine and

ROMAN EMPIRE AD 14

The century up to the death of Augustus saw the most rapid and continuous expansion in Rome's history. A series of gifted commanders at the head of the new professional legions carved out fresh provinces in Europe, Africa and the East. During these years Roman soldiers crossed the Rhine and Euphrates, reached the Elbe, explored the deserts south of Egypt, pushed around the shores of the Black Sea, and landed in Britain.

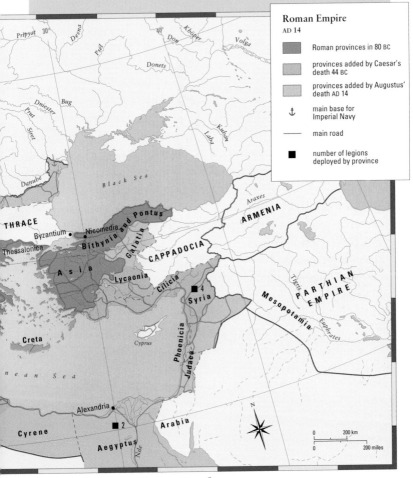

Roman Empire
AD 14

- Roman provinces in 80 BC
- provinces added by Caesar's death 44 BC
- provinces added by Augustus' death AD 14
- ⚓ main base for Imperial Navy
- — main road
- ■ number of legions deployed by province

Danube in Europe, and the Euphrates in the East. Apart from a few later additions, the basic shape which the Roman Empire was to maintain for over four centuries had already been established. This chapter will tell the story of these vast conquests. It will also describe how the citizen militia of the Republic changed into a professional army of long-service soldiers recruited from the marginal elements of society.

Before considering how the Romans created this vast Empire, it is worth pausing to discuss *why* they did so. For a long time it was believed that the Romans were not willing imperialists, but had been drawn on to fight war after war to defend themselves and their allies against real or imagined threats. This view was most popular at the beginning of the twentieth century when the great European empires still held sway over most of the globe, and the rule and improving influence of the civilized over the uncivilized was accepted as an inherently good thing. It was attractive when emphasizing the benefits of Roman civilization to view the acquisition of their Empire as accidental, rather than motivated by a blatant desire for power and wealth. In the last few decades, when the memories of empire seem so distant, a generation of scholars for whom imperialism is associated not with progress, but with exploitation and repression of indigenous cultures, have adopted a far more hostile attitude to Roman expansion. They have claimed that Roman society was geared towards annual aggressive warfare, and concentrated in particular on the requirement of the aristocracy for military adventures.

The men who governed Rome's provinces and commanded her armies were senators following a well-defined career pattern, known as the *cursus honorum*, which involved a mixture of civilian and military posts. War and politics were inseparably linked at Rome. Politicians did not advocate specific policies or belong to anything resembling modern political parties, but were elected to magistracies largely on their own and their family's reputation; the system favoured the members of the old aristocratic families who could boast of the great achievements of their ancestors. The numbers in each college of magistrates declined in proportion with its seniority, and only a small minority of the Senate's 300 members could ever hope to hold one of the two annual consulships. Competition was fierce to gain election, and then even more intense to achieve distinction during a man's year of office, so that he returned to assume the influential place in the Senate befitting his great reputation. The greatest prestige came from military success, and a magistrate who had held supreme command in a victorious war won the right to celebrate a triumph, riding in a chariot through Rome to the acclamation of the whole city. Even the men who had achieved this honour vied with each other to stage the most spectacular triumph, or to build the greatest monument and stage the most lavish games to commemorate it. Flamininus, Scipio Asiaticus, Manlius Vulso and Aemilius Paullus, all of whom had fought successful wars in the Hellenistic east, were each credited with staging a triumph that was greater than any that had preceded it. Each one had also to stave off political attacks from rivals who did not wish them to receive the honour.

A provincial governor usually had only a single campaigning season in which to fight a successful war before he was replaced by another man equally ambitious for a military adventure. Many arrived in their province impoverished by an expensive election campaign and needing a quick profit. The booty of a victory was considerable, especially in the richer east, and there were always captives to sell into slavery. Returning to Rome, the successful commander displayed his prestige in the size and splendour of his house in Rome and his servile household, and invested in vast rural estates worked by a labour force of slaves. Competition for status among the Roman aristocracy demanded frequent warfare, and it is not surprising that some Roman generals provoked a war for their personal glory. Gnaeus Manlius Vulso arrived to take over the army in Asia after the victory at Magnesia. Having vainly tried to provoke Antiochus to break the peace and restart the war, in 189 BC he launched an unprovoked attack on the Galatians, three Celtic tribes who had settled in Asia Minor a century before. On his return to Italy he was criticized for fighting a war without the approval of the Senate and People of Rome, and only narrowly escaped condemnation after mobilizing all his friends and relatives among the senators. In this view Roman expansion was the result of a never-ending search for fresh peoples to defeat and loot in order to supply the aristocracy's demand for wealth and glory, and maintain a constant supply of the slaves on which the economy of Italy had become based.

There were blatant examples of such triumph hunting, but its extent should not be exaggerated. Some provinces offered plenty of opportunities for fighting a campaign which could be presented as being in Rome's interest. The frequency of small-scale warfare against Spanish, Thracian and Gallic tribes led to a law being passed stipulating that at least 5,000 opponents needed to have been killed in battle for the victorious commander to be eligible for a triumph. However, the culture of the Roman aristocracy did not always lead to constant annual war making, and some consuls seem to have made little effort to secure themselves a military command. Competition among senators sometimes had the effect of curbing expansion. The Roman constitution was based around the principle that no one element in the state, and certainly no single politician, should hold overwhelming power. Magistracies were held for only a year, and there was always at least one colleague of equal rank. While politicians were eager to add to their own reputation, they were even more keen to prevent rivals from gaining too much influence.

There is much truth in this picture of senators as inherently aggressive, but it is far too simplistic as an explanation for Roman imperialism. Rome may have appeared geared to constant annual warfare, but in fact the intensity of Roman war making and expansion varied immensely. There were periods of several decades during the second century BC when very few wars were fought, and then only on a small scale, and much of the great territorial expansion occurred in short, intense bursts. The Romans were not unusual in fighting frequent wars, but the relentless quality of their war making was distinctive. As we have seen in the last chapter, a Roman war could only end when the enemy ceased to be a threat, having either been absorbed as a subordinate ally or destroyed as a political entity. If this outcome was not fully achieved in a single war, then further conflicts were almost inevitable until the Romans had achieved their aim.

The Romans provoked the Third Punic War (149–146 BC) and utterly destroyed Carthage when they felt that she was starting to re-emerge as an independent power, having finally paid off the indemnity of the Second Punic War. A defeated enemy did not necessarily need to be annexed and turned into a province. In fact the Romans were reluctant to establish new provinces and increase the number of overseas garrisons supplied by their citizen army. After the Second Macedonian War, the kingdom's power was curbed, but it retained its independence. Following the Third War the kingdom was dissolved and replaced by four self-governing regions. It was only when these regional governments had failed to cope with the invasion of the pretender Andriscus and the Fourth War that the Roman province of Macedonia was created. Nor were the Romans always swift to exploit the resources of their provinces, and it was several decades after the creation of their Spanish provinces that they began to derive much benefit from the area's mineral wealth.

Roman expansion was a complex process which varied in intensity and nature. If one characteristic typifies the Romans (and especially the senators) at this period it was their supreme self-confidence. Roman senators had long come to consider themselves the equal of any foreign king. Their attitude was reflected in the confrontation between the Roman embassy, headed by the ex-consul Gaius Popilius Laenas, and Antiochus IV of Syria in 167 BC. When the Seleucids invaded Egypt, Rome did not send an army to defend her ally, but only a small group of commissioners. When Antiochus politely offered his hand to Popilius, the Roman brusquely thrust a tablet containing the Senate's ultimatum into it. The king, faced with a demand for his immediate withdrawal from Egypt, said that he would discuss the matter with his advisers before giving a reply. The impatient Popilius used the point of his staff to draw in the dust, enclosing Antiochus in a circle and

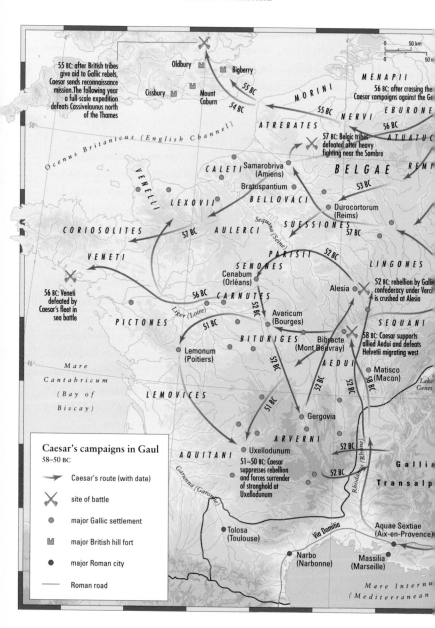

55 BC: after British tribes give aid to Gallic rebels, Caesar sends reconnaissance mission. The following year a full-scale expedition defeats Cassivelaunus north of the Thames

Oldbury

Bigberry

Cissbury

Mount Caburn

55 BC

54 BC

MENAPII

56 BC: after crossing the Caesar campaigns against the Ge

NERVI

EBURONE

MORINI

ATREBATES

55 BC

56 BC

ATUATUC

57 BC: Belgic tribes defeated after heavy fighting near the Sambre

BELGAE

REMI

53 BC

Ocenus Britanicus (English Channel)

VENELLI

CALETI

Samarobriva (Amiens)

Bratuspantium

BELLOVACI

Durocortorum (Reims)

LEXOVII

SUESSIONES

57 BC

CORIOSOLITES

57 BC

AULERCI

Sequana (Seine)

PARISII

52 BC

LINGONES

VENETI

SENONES

Cenabum (Orléans)

Alesia

52 BC: rebellion by Galli confederacy under Verci is crushed at Alesia

56 BC: Veneti defeated by Caesar's fleet in sea battle

56 BC

CARNUTES

52 BC

Liger (Loire)

Avaricum (Bourges)

SEQUANI

PICTONES

51 BC

BITURIGES

Bibracte (Mont Beuvray)

58 BC: Caesar supports allied Aedui and defeats Helvetii migrating west

Lemonum (Poitiers)

52 BC

AEDUI

Matisco (Macon)

Lake Genet

Mare Cantabricum (Bay of Biscay)

LEMOVICES

51 BC

52 BC

57 BC

57 BC

58 BC

Gergovia

Caesar's campaigns in Gaul
58–50 BC

ARVERNI

52 BC

Galli

Transalp

Caesar's route (with date)

AQUITANI

Uxellodunum

51–50 BC: Caesar suppresses rebellion and forces surrender of stronghold at Uxellodunum

52 BC

Rhodanus (Rhône)

site of battle

major Gallic settlement

major British hill fort

major Roman city

Roman road

Garumna (Garonne)

Tolosa (Toulouse)

Via Domitia

Aquae Sextiae (Aix-en-Provence)

Narbo (Narbonne)

Massilia (Marseille)

Mare Internu (Mediterranean)

demanding an answer before he stepped out of it. The astonished king accepted the terms without question. The Roman attitude to foreign powers was often high-handed, frequently reverting to the use or threat of force.

NORTHERN ITALY

In 225 BC the last great Gallic raid into central Italy was trapped between two consular armies and destroyed. For the next fifty years the Romans assumed the offensive against the Celtic tribes of that area of northern Italy known as Cisalpine Gaul. Hannibal's arrival encouraged renewed hostility, and one Carthaginian officer, Hamilcar, continued to lead the tribes against Rome for several years after the Second Punic War, until he was killed in battle. The fighting in Cisalpine Gaul, only a few hundred kilometres from Rome, was closely supervised by the Senate, which committed considerable resources of manpower to the subjugation of the area.

Battles fought against the Gallic tribes were in many ways similar to those fought against Carthaginian or Hellenistic opponents. There were the same delays and ritual challenges before a battle, each side reluctant to risk combat until every possible advantage had been gained. Normally the Roman

CAESAR'S CAMPAIGNS IN GAUL

Benefiting from a political alliance with Pompey and Crassus, Julius Caesar was able to secure an extraordinary ten-year command of the two Gallic provinces and Illyria. Early interventions in Gallia Comata ('hairy Gaul', the area outside the Roman province) against the migrating Helvetii and the German war leader Ariovistus, led on to further conflicts with more distant tribes, till Caesar's legions had subdued the whole area. To attract public attention at Rome, Caesar staged two expeditions to the mysterious island of Britain. He was to face two major rebellions, one in the winter of 54–53 BC amongst the Belgic tribes and another a year later uniting much of Gaul under the leadership of Vercingetorix.

generals outclassed Gallic leaders in this tentative manoeuvring much as Hannibal had outclassed the first Romans sent against him. Tribal armies were clumsy and it was difficult for their leaders to manoeuvre them during a battle. They were composed of two elements: the warrior bands supported by each nobleman and the mass of the ordinary tribesmen. Noblemen displayed their status by the numbers and fame of the warriors who lived at their expense under an obligation to fight for them. These bands were semi-permanent and provided a well-equipped and highly motivated nucleus to any Gallic army. They were far outnumbered by the mass of ordinary warriors composed of all free tribesmen able to equip themselves, and loosely grouped by family and clan relationships. Gallic leaders fought at the head of their followers, inspiring them by their personal prowess. Tactics were simple, and relied on a headlong charge by a screaming mass of warriors. The first charge of a Gallic army was a dreadful thing, but the Romans believed that if they could withstand this onslaught then the Gauls would steadily tire and become vulnerable. Classical literature claims that the barbarians were poorly conditioned and easily tired by strenuous activity and heat. But probably the main reason why the Romans were likely to win a prolonged combat was their *triplex acies* formation that allowed them to reinforce threatened parts of the line. Individually the Romans were better equipped and armoured than the majority of Celtic warriors, but there is little indication of the great superiority which Caesar's troops in the first century BC would display against similar Gallic opponents. Gallic armies did successfully ambush Roman columns on the march, for instance destroying most of the army commanded by the praetor Lucius Postumius in 216 BC, but this was only possible when the Gauls had had enough time to muster their whole army along the likely route of the Roman advance. Mustering a Gallic army and then deploying it for battle was a slow procedure, and it is notable that very often tribes were unable to form an army until the Romans had attacked their territory, ravaged their fields and then begun to withdraw.

One heavy defeat in battle was usually enough to force a Hellenistic monarch to seek terms. Each Gallic tribe was separate and had to be defeated in turn. A victory over a neighbouring tribe might overawe other peoples, but it did not in itself force them to capitulate. When every free male in the tribe was able to fight as a warrior, battle casualties were easier to absorb than among professional armies. Not only that, but the tribes themselves were divided into clans and factions. Most included a number of powerful chieftains or sub-kings, one of whom might be recognized as the monarch of the whole tribe. Each leader headed a faction within the tribe which would grow or decline depending on his achievements, and the numbers of warriors whom he attracted to any expedition varied according to his reputation. A peace negotiated with a tribe did not guarantee the acceptance of all its members. Warfare played a central role in Gallic society. Leaders needed wealth to support their band of followers and the most common way of gaining this was by raiding. Raids and counter-raids figured heavily in the campaigns in Cisalpine Gaul. A favourite target for the Celts were the colonies which the Romans had settled north of the Po, and these were frequently beleaguered and sometimes sacked.

The settlement of large numbers of citizens in colonies in Cisalpine Gaul was an unusual feature of Roman imperialism at this period. Their presence was an added source of friction with the Gauls and Ligurians, as the settlers pressed for more land and divided up confiscated tribal territory into regular squares by the Roman process of centuriation. They emphasized the permanence of Roman occupation, as did the roads that were constructed. Earlier Roman roads had always begun at Rome itself, linking the city directly to a new area of settlement. In 187 BC the Via Aemilia was constructed connecting the two colonies of Arminum and Placentia, the first Roman road designed to be excessively straight. A straight line may be the shortest distance between two points, but it is seldom the easiest route, and a road stretching straight from one horizon to the next was a

The Via Appia connecting Rome with Capua and the Campanian plain was built in 312 BC under the orders of the censor, Appius Claudius Caecus. An important aspect of Rome's absorption of conquered territory was the construction of roads linking new colonies to Rome and, increasingly, to each other.

powerful statement of control over conquered territory. It was also, in that characteristically Roman way of combining the impressive and the practical, a valuable means of strategic movement. The process of consolidating and organizing the province continued throughout the century, converting individual settlements linked to Rome into a coherent unit. At the same time, the Romans' attitude towards their Empire as a whole began to change, and it gradually began to assume a greater air of permanence. At first each province was viewed as distinct and individually connected to Rome. In 171 BC, at the beginning of the Third Macedonian War, both consuls had hoped to be given command against Perseus, and the unsuccessful man had been sent with an army to the frontier with Illyria to protect colonists in the area. This man, Cassius Longinus, decided on his own initiative to march his army overland to Macedonia. By chance the Senate heard of his expedition and were able to send a commission to restrain him. On the one hand this is just another example of the Roman aristocracy's lust for glory affecting their behaviour in the provinces, but it also shows that the Romans were beginning to conceive of their provinces as being linked to each other geographically. In the last decades of the century, the Romans mounted a series of campaigns to defeat the tribes of southern Gaul, creating the province of Transalpine Gaul (modern Provence) to provide a secure land route to their Spanish provinces. Gradually a coherent empire began to emerge from a collection of individual conquered peoples.

SPAIN

After the Second Punic War Rome maintained a permanent military presence in Spain to ensure that a second Hannibal could not use it as a base for an invasion of Italy. Spain was populated by three main groups: the Lusitanians in the west, Iberians in the south and east and the Celtiberians in the north. Tribal groupings were looser than in Gaul and each small fortified town was effectively independent. Divisions were common within communities and leaders tended to enjoy power for only as long as they were militarily successful. There were no real equivalents to the kings of Gallic tribes. There were many misunderstandings as the Romans attempted to negotiate with authorities whom they believed spoke for an entire community, only to discover that this was not so. On one occasion a Roman commander was attacked and his baggage plundered by warriors from a tribe with which he had just concluded a treaty. Soon afterwards a contingent of cavalry from the same tribe arrived to serve as auxiliaries in his army as had been agreed in the treaty. The confused Romans held them responsible for the raid and had them put in chains. Spanish society was difficult to understand for men who only served for one year in the provinces. The fragmentation of social and political structures in Spain had been exacerbated by decades of warfare as first the Carthaginians and then the Romans had fought to establish their power in the region. A growing population worsened the situation, particularly as a career of mercenary service with Carthage was no longer available to landless young men.

Raiding and banditry became more frequent. Continual warfare hindered agriculture, which in turn encouraged more communities to supplement their living by raiding others. Groups of landless men banded together to raid the surrounding communities. The motivation for this activity was brutally pragmatic. If a community was perceived to be weak it would be attacked, if strong then it would be avoided or alliance sought with it. Raid provoked counter-raid to maintain a continuous cycle of plundering which might easily escalate into formal battles. The Romans attempted to construct a network of allied peoples to create stability in their Spanish provinces. To preserve this they needed to prevent or avenge any raids on their allies. Failure to do so, or a Roman defeat, however small, encouraged more widespread attacks and allied tribes to defect.

One solution was to resettle the landless warriors elsewhere. The Romans had done something similar with the Ligurians, a mountain people of north-west Italy who possessed an even more disparate and fragmented political structure than the Spaniards. Large numbers of Ligurians had been forcibly deported, settled on fertile land elsewhere in Italy and turned into stable and peaceful farmers. In 150 BC the governor of Further Spain, Servius Sulpicius Galba, accepted the surrender of a band of Lusitanians and promised to provide them with plots of land in a fertile area. The Lusitanians had been plundering the Roman province for several years, inflicting several defeats on Roman forces. Defeated by the previous governor and forced to accept peace, the tribes had

The Gallic hill town of Roquepertuse was sacked by the Romans in the 120s BC. It included this important shrine, decorated with severed heads set into niches in the wall. Head-hunting was practised by many of the peoples of Iron Age Europe, but was especially important to the Gauls, whose religion invested the head with great importance.

returned to raiding after his departure, excusing this breach of a treaty by claiming that poverty forced them to attack their neighbours. Galba disarmed the warriors, divided them and their families into three groups and then ordered his troops to massacre them all. On his return to Rome, Galba was prosecuted for breaking faith with the Lusitanians, but was acquitted after mobilizing his relations in the Senate and, in a desperate gesture, bringing his weeping children into the court in an effort to invoke the pity of the jury. Galba went on to become one of the most famous orators of his day, but never again commanded an army. A similar atrocity had been committed in the other Spanish province a few years before when the praetor Lucullus had launched an unprovoked attack on a tribe, accepted their surrender and then massacred them. These were both examples of Roman behaviour at its worst, yet the two commanders evaded prosecution. Such incidents lend support to the idea of the Romans as brutal imperialists, individual governors seeking out vulnerable foreign peoples to butcher for the loot and glory. They are also indications of the frustration felt by many Roman commanders at the apparent impossibility of winning a permanent victory in Spain. The events of the next decades were to reinforce this opinion.

One of the few survivors of Galba's massacre was a Lusitanian named Viriathus, who was soon to emerge as an inspirational leader and a skilled commander, defeating or evading all the Roman forces sent against him. He is an example of the type of charismatic leader who often appeared after the initial stages of Roman conquest had destroyed traditional power structures in an area. Other examples would include Vercingetorix in Gaul and Arminius in Germany, both of whom were able to lead very large armies drawn from confederations of tribes. The basis of their power was personal and tended to collapse as soon as the leader disappeared from the scene. Viriathus was murdered by a treacherous subordinate who hoped for reward from Rome. The Emperor Tiberius would later refuse an offer made by a German chieftain to assassinate Arminius, but only because successful Roman campaigns had checked the latter's power and removed any threat he posed. In other circumstances, when the continuance of a conflict rested solely on the perseverance of a single leader, the Romans arranged the treacherous capture of Jugurtha of Numidia in 106 BC or mounted attacks with the primary objective of killing the enemy commander.

Encouraged by Viriathus' successes, another rebellion against Rome had developed in northern Spain, centred around the city of Numantia. Large but poorly led and unprepared Roman armies advanced against the rebels and suffered disaster. An army commanded by Gaius Hostilius Mancinus was surrounded by the Celtiberians and forced to surrender in 137 BC, the Romans accepting peace on equal terms to the Numantines. The Senate refused to ratify the treaty and sent back Mancinus, naked and in chains, to the Numantines, who refused to receive him. The Romans elected Scipio Aemilianus, the man who had destroyed Carthage, to a second consulship and gave him the command in Spain. Scipio carefully retrained the troops in the province and added to the men he had brought with him, leading an army of sixty thousand men against the Numantines. Despite his great numerical superiority, he refused to face the eight thousand Numantines in battle, so great was the advantage in morale they had gained over the Roman troops. Instead, he blockaded Numantia, building a wall strengthened by forts to surround the city. After a long struggle, in which the starving

This battle scene from the Arch of Orange commemorates the defeat of one of the occasional Gallic rebellions that occurred in the seventy years after Caesar's conquest. Probably dating to the reign of Tiberius, it provides an excellent depiction of the equipment worn by legionaries and auxiliary cavalrymen in the early first century AD.

defenders are alleged to have resorted to cannibalism, the Numantines surrendered and the city was destroyed in 133 BC. The fall of Numantia marked the end of intensive campaigning in Spain, although the peninsula was not fully pacified for more than a century.

THE RISE OF THE PROFESSIONAL ARMY

The second half of the second century BC was a sorry chapter in Roman military history. Viriathus and the Numantines humiliated successive Roman armies in Spain, and the only major defeat of the Macedonian wars occurred in 149 BC when a motley army of Thracians led by a pretender to the throne defeated a Roman force and killed the praetor in command. Rome had provoked the Third Punic War out of fear that Carthage was rebuilding her strength, but the opening of the campaign in Africa saw badly trained and poorly led Roman soldiers suffering one disaster after another. The Romans eventually won all of these conflicts, and the utter destruction of

Carthage in 146 BC conformed to the trend of Roman warfare becoming simultaneously more brutal and less successful. The atrocities committed in Spain in the 150s have already been mentioned, and it is probable that Polybius' description of the violence of the Roman sack of a city, where not only people but even dogs were slaughtered and mutilated, was most typical of this period. This ferocity was a product of frustration at the difficulty of achieving complete victory, and fear produced by many unexpected defeats.

Nearly every campaign in the rest of the century followed the same pattern of early disasters before a prolonged effort brought victory. The war with the Numidian king Jugurtha (112–106 BC) resulted in scandals as troops deserted en masse, and commanders were found to be either incompetent or had been bribed by the enemy. The first Roman army sent to the war surrendered and suffered the humiliation of being sent under the yoke. The migrating Germanic tribes of the Cimbri and Teutones threatened Italy itself after they had smashed a series of Roman armies sent against them. The casualties at Arausio in 105 BC were on the same scale as those at Cannae, with allegedly eighty

A Roman copy of a Hellenistic original, the Dying Gaul is one of the finest pieces of Classical art, symbolizing both the splendour of barbarian races and their inevitable defeat by civilization. The long moustache and the limed hair, combed up to create an intimidating, spiky effect, are common in literary descriptions of Celts, as is the heroic nudity.

thousand men falling. Alarm at the prospect of a repeat of the Gallic sack caused such panic that for the last time in their history the Romans performed a human sacrifice, burying alive a Greek and a Gallic man and woman in the forum.

A major factor in these disasters was Roman overconfidence. The defeat of the kingdoms of the Hellenistic world, the conquest of Cisalpine Gaul and the wars up to Gracchus' settlement in Spain were all fought by armies and commanders raised in the hard school of the war with Hannibal. The intense campaigning of the first quarter of the century was followed by a relatively peaceful twenty-five years, broken only by the Third Macedonian War. Gradually the collected experience of the generation of the Second Punic War was lost. A new generation grew up who had forgotten that the earlier successes were the result of careful preparation and training, and assumed that victory came as a matter of course, simply because they were Roman. Fewer of the ordinary soldiers were veterans and many of their inexperienced officers either thought that it was unnecessary or did not know how to turn them into effective units. If soldiers had served in other campaigns they were as likely to have experienced defeats as victories. Many of the successes of Viriathus and the Numantines were won over more numerous Roman forces.

The changing situation placed a great strain on the militia system as permanent garrisons needed to be maintained in many of the overseas provinces.

The old ideal of the citizen farmer, who owned enough property to equip himself as a soldier and served for a campaigning season before returning to till his fields, was under threat. Such a man faced ruination if he was unable to tend his land for a decade of service in a legion in Spain. In the latter part of the second century Romans believed that the numbers of citizens owning enough land to qualify them for military service was dwindling. Increasingly large stretches of Italy had been swallowed up by great estates (or *latifundia*), owned by aristocrats enriched by Roman expansion and worked by gangs of slaves captured in foreign wars. Scholarly opinion remains divided over the real extent of this problem, some claiming that free yeoman farmers were flourishing in some parts of Italy, but it is clear that the Romans believed their previously inexhaustible supply of military manpower was under threat. Even if the number of potential recruits had not fallen by that much, the numerous setbacks suffered by Roman armies may well have created the impression that their quality had declined.

Traditionally, Marius, the general who won the war with Jugurtha and then defeated the Cimbri, has been credited with converting the Roman army from a militia raised through universal conscription, into a professional army recruited from volunteers. Certainly, before leaving to take command of the army in Africa, Marius appealed for volunteers from the class known as the *capite censi* (citizens who did not possess enough property to make them liable to service in the legions). More recently, scholars have interpreted the change as occurring gradually, pointing to earlier measures to reduce the minimum qualification for service and equip soldiers at the state's expense. There do appear to have been some men who viewed military service as a career before these changes. Livy tells us of one such 'professional' soldier, Spurius Ligustinus, who first enrolled in the army in 200 BC and had served twenty-two years in Greece and Spain before his re-enlistment for the Third Macedonian War. Highly decorated, Ligustinus had served all but two years as a centurion, holding increasingly senior posts, culminating in that of *primus pilus*. His pattern of service would not have been much out of place in the army of the Empire, and in fact Livy presents his career in a style suspiciously similar to the memorial inscriptions that were beginning to become popular with soldiers in the late first century BC. Ligustinus is presented as the ideal farmer soldier, since Livy takes care to point out that he still farmed the plot of land he had been left by his father, where his wife had borne him six sons and two daughters. What is interesting is that this smallholding was not of sufficient size to have rendered him liable to military service at all, and that his army service had been voluntary.

How common such semi-professionals were is impossible to estimate, nor can we know whether most such men were to be found among the centurionate rather than the rank and file.

Although we cannot precisely trace the process of change, the character of the army had changed irrevocably by the first century BC. The soldiers were now recruited mainly from the landless poor, men for whom military service was a career rather than a temporary interlude in their normal occupation. After the Social War, which saw the last great rebellion of some of Rome's Italian allies, Roman citizenship was extended to much of the Italian peninsula. The old *alae* disappeared and all Italians were now recruited into the legions. These legions became more permanent, and began to develop a distinct identity, a process accelerated by Marius' replacement of the five standards of a legion (a boar, a wolf, a horse, an eagle and a minotaur) with a single silver eagle. All the old distinctions based on property and age were swept away. The cavalry and *velites* disappeared and all legionaries were now heavy infantry armed with the *pilum* and *gladius*, wearing mail armour, a bronze helmet and carrying a long, oval shield. The main tactical sub-unit of the legion was now the cohort instead of the maniple. Each of a legion's ten cohorts consisted of 480 men divided into three maniples, each of two centuries of eighty men commanded by a centurion. The six tribunes were still the senior officers permanently attached to a unit, but it became increasingly common for one of the army commander's staff, often a senior subordinate or *legatus*, to be in effective command. The origins of the cohort are obscure. Polybius mentions the term twice, both in connection with Scipio's army in Spain in the Second Punic War and in an ambiguous passage maybe implying that it consisted of three maniples, as was later to be the case. Livy uses the term anachronistically, but we do know that allied contingents were usually called cohorts, although we do not know their size or internal structure. It is possible that a cohort was a term for any unit smaller than a legion, but larger than a maniple. The cohort appears to have been adopted on an *ad hoc* basis by the legions in Spain during the second century BC. Much of the campaigning in Spain was on a relatively small scale, when each community might have to be defeated in turn. The old lines of the manipular legion were not effective tactical units for independent operations. The cohort, with its own command structure and with men used to working together, may well have fulfilled a need for forces smaller than a legion.

The new legion was more flexible in every respect than its predecessor. Its usual formation was in the *triplex acies* with the cohorts deployed in the *quincunx* pattern, but it could as effectively deploy into one, two or four lines. The uniformly equipped and sized cohorts could be deployed anywhere, unlike the maniples which had been restricted to fixed positions. It was much easier for a commander to control and pass orders to ten cohorts each with their own commanders than it was to do the same with thirty maniples. Roman armies had always become more efficient through long service, training and experience of success, but the greater permanence of the new legions made it easier to preserve this accumulated experience. With professionalization Roman armies began to show far greater ability in the more technical aspects of warfare. Caesar could call from the ranks of his legions men able to design and build bridges or ships, and engineers to prosecute a siege. The average efficiency of Roman armies greatly increased and campaigns were less often delayed when experienced legions had to be discharged and replaced by newly raised units.

There was a major disadvantage to the new system. The professional soldier was recruited from the poor and had no source of livelihood once he was discharged from the army. The Senate refused to take responsibility for demobilized soldiers and made no provision for them or their families, since by law the armies were still supposed to be filled with men of property serving out of duty. The army ceased to represent the whole Roman people under arms and became more and more separate from the rest of society, their loyalty focusing more on their legion than on Rome. Soldiers came to depend on their commanders to provide them with a plot of land on discharge. Charismatic generals

Trajan's Column pays particular attention to the technical skills of the citizen legionaries. The willingness and skill with which the professional legions undertook major works of engineering was one of the most remarkable features of the Roman army. During his campaigns, Caesar was able to draw from the ranks of his army men able to construct great systems of fortifications, build and repair ships, and bridge the River Rhine.

such as Sulla, Pompey and Caesar created armies far more loyal to their leaders than they were to the state. This added an increasingly violent dimension to Rome's competitive politics. The professional armies were as often set to fight against other legions as they were against the foreign enemies of Rome.

The Great Conquests

During the second century the profits of empire had not been evenly distributed, and the gap between the richest and poorest senators became steadily wider. Frequent military setbacks encouraged the appointment of the ablest commanders to take charge for the duration

CIVIL WARS

Rome's greatest period of expansion coincided with and was intimately linked to a series of violent civil wars as various successful commanders vied for supremacy. These campaigns were fought not just in Italy, but all around the Mediterranean. Caesar failed as dictator to establish a permanent peace and it was only after another thirteen years of war that his nephew and adopted son Octavian managed to bring a lasting peace from civil war to the exhausted Empire.

of a conflict. Marius was given the command in Africa by popular demand, and then elected to five successive consulships to combat the Cimbri. Such continuity of command was militarily sound and had been employed at times of crisis in the past, notably the Second Punic War, but it struck at the very heart of the Roman political system which required all power to be temporary. Such prolonged commands brought massive profits to the commander, raising him far above his peers in the Senate. Competition in the Senate became focused on a small group of the foremost politicians, who now expected to be given such wide-ranging commands as a right, regardless of whether a military crisis threatened the Empire. When Sulla earned the dubious distinction of being the first man to march his legions against Rome in 88 BC, it was because he had been replaced by his rival Marius in the command of the major war against the kingdom of Pontus. Civil wars encouraged even more exceptional careers among those who supported the winning side. While the annual replacement of provincial governors may have encouraged frequent campaigns, this lack of continuity had not given any encouragement to wide-scale, planned expansion. The powerful generals in the

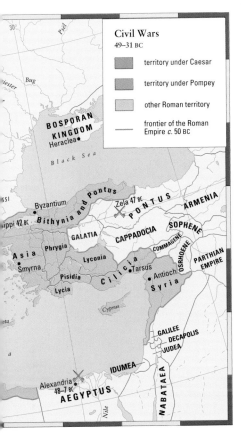

Civil Wars
49–31 BC

- territory under Caesar
- territory under Pompey
- other Roman territory
- frontier of the Roman Empire c. 50 BC

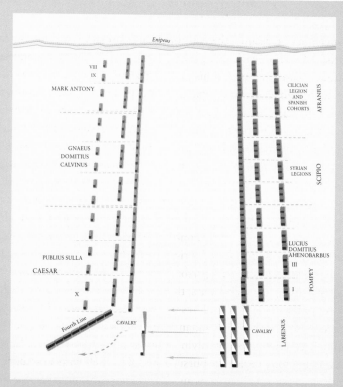

Enipeus

VIII
IX
MARK ANTONY

GNAEUS
DOMITIUS
CALVINUS

PUBLIUS SULLA
CAESAR

X

Fourth Line   CAVALRY

CILICIAN
LEGION
AND
SPANISH
COHORTS

AFRANIUS

SYRIAN
LEGIONS

SCIPIO

LUCIUS
DOMITIUS
AHENOBARBUS
III

I

POMPEY

CAVALRY

LABIENUS

The Battle of Pharsalus, 9th August 48 BC

Pharsalus is described in considerable detail by our sources, allowing us to depict the troop deployments down to cohort level. The battle showed the flexibility of the Roman tactical system, especially when employed by a veteran army under a commander of Caesar's ability. Pompey hoped to use his numerically superior cavalry to smash through Caesar's horse on the right wing and envelop his infantry. Seeing the danger, Caesar took one cohort from the third line of each legion and formed a separate fourth line behind his own cavalry. The Pompeian horse lost much of their order as they drove off their opposite numbers, and were stampeded to the rear in panic when the fourth line suddenly counter-attacked. Threatened now on their left by Caesar's victorious cohorts, and under steady pressure from the front, Pompey's legions gradually began to crumble and finally collapsed into rout.

first century BC secured the control of large provinces and armies for periods of several years, giving themselves far more scope for conquest.

Caesar's own accounts of his campaigns give us an invaluable picture of the Roman army on campaign in this period. Caesar did little to reform the army, but raised the troops under his command to the peak of efficiency. The booty from the Gallic campaigns was lavishly distributed among the soldiers, and conspicuous service was rewarded by decorations and rapid promotion. Newly raised legions were provided with a valuable cadre of experienced centurions promoted from junior grades in veteran units. Caesar trained his men hard, but also flattered them, fostering their pride in themselves and their unit. He created an especially close bond with the veteran Tenth Legion, habitually placing them on the right of his line, the position of most honour, and leading them in person. When this legion, worn out by long service in foreign and civil wars, threatened to mutiny, Caesar restored order with a single word, addressing them as '*Quirites*', civilians not soldiers. A highly active commander, Caesar took care to prepare his campaigns scrupulously, involving himself in many of the details, but once operations began he pursued his objectives with unremitting boldness, trusting to his troops and his own improvisational genius and good luck to cope with any crisis. Modern commentators have criticized Caesar for his recklessness, failing to make adequate preparations for his landings in Britain or invading Macedonia against much stronger opposition during the civil war, but this is to misunderstand the doctrine of the Roman army. Roman commanders were habitually bold in their actions, and if a Roman army did not seek to seize the initiative and act aggressively, then it was usually a sign that things were going very badly. The boldness of Caesar's campaigns was not markedly greater than those of many Roman commanders, and certainly no different from the campaigns of Lucullus or Pompey.

Caesar's behaviour as a commander was typically Roman, although in his own accounts of his campaigns he is careful to show that he was better than anyone else at everything. Before his battles we find the same cautious manoeuvring to gain every slight advantage that we have seen from the third century onwards. This was particularly so in the battles of the civil war when he was careful to show his reluctance to shed the blood of fellow citizens. During a battle Caesar rode around, close behind the front line of his army. From this position he encouraged his men, witnessed their behaviour and rewarded or punished them accordingly. He also had a close view of the combat and could gauge how the fighting was going, judging from the appearance of confidence of each side and the noise they made. Using this information he could send a message to his troops in reserve, or go in person to lead them up to exploit a success or relieve a part of the line that was under pressure. This was the normal way of commanding a Roman army, practised from at least the end of the third century BC into late antiquity. A good general needed to judge where and when the crisis of a battle would occur and move to that part of the line. By Caesar's day each legion was controlled by a senior officer, usually a legate; larger armies were divided into a centre and two wings, each led by a senior subordinate, who commanded that sector in the same style as the commander-in-chief. These men were trusted to use their initiative if a crisis occurred when the general was involved elsewhere on the field. Commanding so close to the fighting was a dangerous practice, exposing the general to missiles and being singled out for the attacks of especially bold enemies. However, it did allow a commander to have far more influence on the course of the battle than a general who fought in person in the front rank, or one who surveyed the action from a safe location far in the rear. That the Romans developed a military system which placed such demands on the commander disproves the traditional view that most Roman generals were 'amateurs' of limited ability. The knowledge that their commander shared many of the risks of combat helped to inspire legionaries. Caesar's own account of the critical situation at Sambre in 57 BC well reflects his style of command:

After addressing Legio X, Caesar hurried to the right wing, where he saw his men hard pressed, and the standards of Legio XII clustered in one place and the soldiers so crowded together that it impeded their fighting. All the centurions in the fourth cohort had fallen, the *signifer* was dead and his standard captured; in the remaining cohorts every centurion was either dead or wounded, including the *primus pilus* Sextus Julius Baculus, an exceptionally brave man, who was exhausted by his many serious wounds and could no longer stand; the other soldiers were tired and some in the rear, giving up the fight, were withdrawing out of missile range; the enemy were edging closer up the slope in front and pressing hard on both flanks. He saw that the situation was critical and that there was no other reserve available, took a shield from a man in the rear ranks – he had come without his own – advanced into the front line and called on the centurions by name, encouraged the soldiers, and ordered the line to advance and the units to extend, so that they could employ their swords more easily. His arrival brought hope to the soldiers and refreshed their spirits, every man wanting to do his best in the sight of his general even in such a desperate situation. The enemy's advance was delayed for a while. (*Bellum Gallicum*, 2. 25.)

It is worth noting that Caesar, although he had moved into the front line, does not bother to tell us whether or not he actually fought hand-to-hand. What he does stress is that he exposed himself to danger in order more effectively to do his job of encouraging his centurions and soldiers and reorganizing their battle line. The general's job was to lead and control his army, not inspire them with his personal prowess, like the warrior aristocrats of early Rome or Alexander the Great, who consciously emulated the behaviour of Homeric heroes. *Virtus* was the word used to describe the military virtues which a Roman senator was expected to display because of his birth and upbringing. *Virtus* included the practical ability to lead and control an army, the physical courage needed to perform this role moving around close behind the battle line and the moral courage never to admit the possibility of defeat. Caesar portrays himself as never doubting his ultimate success, doing his best to extricate his army from any crisis so that it was best fitted to renew any struggle. Even in his rare defeats he never despaired, but did his best to disengage his army from disaster and prepare to fight again at a later time. This was the ideal behaviour for a Roman commander.

THE LAST PHASE OF ROMAN EXPANSION

Civil wars were lost and won in the provinces surrounding the Mediterranean, but it was only possible for peace to be maintained by creating a secure regime in Rome itself. Caesar failed to do this and was stabbed to death in a meeting of the Senate. Only after another period of civil war did his adopted son Octavian at last create a stable regime. Octavian, who was later to be granted the name Augustus by the Senate, created the system known as the Principate, in which he was emperor and monarch in all but name, and reorganized both the army and the provinces. Real power passed to the emperor, but the Senate still provided the governors who ran the Empire and commanded armies in the field. Attempting to disassociate himself from the Octavian who had risen to power through bloody civil war, Augustus made great play of having restored peace to the state, but while he had ended civil war his reign saw constant warfare and expansion against foreign enemies. Roman politicians had always needed military glory and Augustus, who portrayed himself as the greatest of Rome's magistrates, required the prestige of vanquishing great foreign enemies.

During his Principate Augustus complete the final conquest of Spain, Gaul and Illyria and suppressed rebellions. Africa, Egypt and Syria were all pacified and settled in a process which assimilated and digested the vast conquests of the previous century. The last tribes of

The famous Prima Porta statue of Augustus depicts him as a commander. In fact, he was not an especially able soldier, was often in poor health and relied on more gifted subordinates, such as Agrippa and, later, younger members of his own family. The central motif on the breastplate shows a Parthian returning one of the eagles lost by Crassus or Antony, a diplomatic rather than military success.

the Alps who still resisted Roman rule and raided traffic through the passes were finally absorbed. In the west, his armies pushed through the Balkans taking the boundary of the Empire to the Danube. Caesar had been careful to portray the Rhine as the dividing line between the Gallic tribes who were fit to be absorbed and the savage shifting hordes of Germans who were not. Augustus' armies pushed on to the Elbe, explored the Baltic coast and formed a new province in Germany. Augustus served on few of these campaigns in person, but most of the major campaigns were fought by members of his family, such as his old friend and son-in-law Agrippa, his stepsons Tiberius and Drusus, and his grandson Germanicus. By the end of the first century no one from outside the Imperial family was permitted to celebrate a triumph.

Things began to go wrong in the last decade of Augustus' life. In AD 6 the recently conquered Pannonian provinces erupted into rebellion. Large numbers of troops were needed to suppress the rising: Tiberius at one point commanded an army of ten legions, but chose to divide his strength because he felt this was too big an army to control effectively. Casualties were so great and military

This memorial commemorates a centurion who was killed in the Teutonberg Wald in AD 9. The inscription reads, 'Marcus Caelius, son of Titus, member of the Lemonian voting tribe, from Bononia (modern Bologna), senior centurion of the Eighteenth Legion, 53 years of age. He fell in the Varian war. If found, his bones may be interred here. His brother, Publius Caelius, son of Titus, of the Lemonian voting tribe, set this up.' Tacitus claimed that captured tribunes and senior centurions were sacrificed by the German tribesmen. Caelius is depicted carrying the vitis, *the vine staff symbolizing his rank, and wearing his decorations on a leather harness. On his head he wears the wreath of the* corona civica, *the highest of all decorations, given for saving the life of a fellow citizen. Flanking him are the busts of two of his freedmen, who presumably were killed with him.*

service so unpopular in war-weary Italy that Augustus had recourse to the desperate measure of freeing slaves and forming them into special units to send to the front. It took nearly three years to put down the rebellion, and almost as soon as this was completed news arrived of a disaster in Germany. The governor Publius Quinctilius Varus, related by marriage to Agrippa, had been tasked with establishing the administration of the new province. Varus was informed of the beginnings of an uprising, but did not realize that its leader was Arminius, a chieftain of the Cherusci who commanded a contingent of auxiliaries in his own army. Varus reacted as any Roman would have done to a report of rebellion, mustering all available troops and marching immediately to confront the rebels. His forces were not supplied or prepared for a full-scale campaign, and his columns were encumbered by the soldiers' families and an unwieldy baggage train, but Varus hoped that a show of force would convince the rebels to surrender. He had carried out a similar operation with much success in the year 4 BC when as governor of Syria he had marched into Judaea and quelled the disorder following the death of Herod the Great. This time he led his three legions into a carefully prepared ambush. Arminius, who had deserted to the rebels early in the campaign, led the German tribesmen in a series of ambushes as Varus' clumsy column made its way along a narrow path through the difficult terrain of the Teutonburg Wald. Unable to deploy and force the enemy to fight an open battle, the Romans were whittled down. Varus did what no Roman commander should have done – he despaired, taking his own life. His army was massacred almost to a man. The disaster in Germany marked the end of the great period of Roman expansion, although it was not its main cause. Over the next decade, several Roman armies crossed the Rhine and exacted a bloody revenge for the destruction of Varus' three legions, but there was never a concerted attempt to recreate a German province to the east of the river.

T FLAVIS BASSV:

F DANSALA EQ A

ORVTVR FABI PV

N XXXXI STP X

CHAPTER FOUR

Controlling the World AD 14–193

The tombstone of Titus Flavius Bassus, an auxiliary cavalryman in the ala Noricorum, *who died at the age of 41 after twenty-six years service. Bassus is depicted in the classic posture of cavalry tombstones in the early Empire, galloping his horse over a cowering and frequently naked barbarian. He wears a long-sleeved tunic, much like the Gallic warrior from Vachères, mail armour and a decorated helmet. To the left stands his servant or groom, carrying two more spears to re-arm his master.*

Controlling the World AD 14–193

THE DYING AUGUSTUS supposedly advised his successor, Tiberius, to maintain the Empire's boundaries in their current position. Rebellions in Pannonia and Germany had shown that a period of consolidation was needed after the decades of conquest, yet subsequent events revealed that the massive expansion of the previous century was never to be repeated. Conquests were made, as when Claudius launched an invasion of Britain in AD 43 or Trajan took Dacia in 101–6. Other annexations, such as Trajan's in Mesopotamia or those of Marcus Aurelius on the Danube, were abandoned only when the emperor died before the new territory had been fully absorbed. The Empire was larger in the early third century BC than in AD 14, but the pace of its expansion had massively diminished.

The reason for this was not primarily military. The Roman Empire was not forced to stop only when it reached enemies which the army could not defeat. Completing the conquest of the German tribes or defeating Parthia was perfectly feasible, given considerable resources in manpower and the determination to pursue a long struggle until victory was attained. The resources may have been lacking in AD 14, after the wars of previous decades, but this was not to remain true for most of the first and second centuries AD. The main reason for the end of Roman expansion was political. The commanders who had led armies to great conquests under the late Republic had also been the main leaders in the civil wars which had destroyed the Republican system of government. The emperor could not afford to allow other senators freedom to conquer, letting them gain prestige, wealth and the personal loyalty of their soldiers so that they became dangerous rivals. The major wars in the latter part of Augustus' Principate had been fought by family members, but few of the later emperors enjoyed such a plentiful supply of relatives whose ability and loyalty could be relied upon. Emperors took care to be present when a great war, especially a war of conquest, was fought. Claudius, lame since birth and denied any military service

Trajan's Column was the centrepiece of the great Forum complex the Emperor built with the spoils of his conquest of Dacia. Around the drum runs a series of reliefs telling the story of Trajan's two Dacian Wars (AD 101–2 and 105–6) in stylized but remarkably detailed images.

as a result, was eager to achieve military glory after his unexpected elevation to the throne, and launched the invasion of Britain. He joined the army when it took the main tribal centre at Camulodunum and accepted the surrender of a crowd of British kings, even though he spent little more than a week in Britain before returning to Rome to celebrate his triumph. More usually, presiding over a great conquest required the emperor to spend a long period away from Rome and many were not secure enough in their position to relish the prospect of this. The system of the Principate did not favour widespread expansion.

THE ARMY OF THE PRINCIPATE

The Julio-Claudian emperors completed the process of converting the Roman army into a professional force of regular soldiers. It was very much the army of the emperor, all recruits taking an oath (the *sacramentum*) of allegiance to the *princeps* rather than the Senate and People of Rome. Regular parades and celebrations were held by all units to commemorate festivals associated with the Imperial family. Images of the emperor, *imagines*, were kept with the standards which symbolized the corporate identity of a unit. When legionaries were discharged they received a bounty and allotment of land paid for through the *Aerarium Militare*, the military treasury established by Augustus and controlled by the emperor. Army commanders were now, with very few exceptions, representatives of the emperor (*legati*) possessed of delegated authority, rather than magistrates holding power in their own name. Decorations for gallantry were awarded in the name of the emperor even if he was far from the theatre of operations.

The legions, about thirty in number by the early second century, remained the principal units of the army. Their paper strength was about 5,240, primarily consisting of ten cohorts of heavy infantry. Each legion included a large number of specialists, such as clerks, engineers, surveyors, artillerymen, weapons' instructors and drill-masters, tent-makers and leather-workers, and craftsmen and artisans connected with the manufacture and repair of weapons and armour. Legions were now permanent, many lasting for well over three hundred years,

and developed a strong sense of identity reflected in their individual numbers and titles. Thus we have Legio XIV Gemina Martia Victrix ('The Twin', probably because of its original formation through the amalgamation of two legions; 'of Mars' or 'martial' and 'Victorious' were titles granted by Nero after its prominent role in the defeat of Boudicca),

THE ROMAN EMPIRE AD 68
Following Nero's suicide in AD 68, the Roman world was plunged into turmoil as four emperors held power in little over a year. In this civil war the Roman divided along provincial lines supporting the various candidates for the throne. The eventual winner was Vespasian, supported at first by the legions in Syria and Judaea, then Egypt and finally most of the Danubian garrisons.

Legio V Alaudae ('The Larks'), Legio VI Ferrata ('The Ironsides') or Legio II Traiana Fortis ('Trajan's own, the strong'). Soldiers tended to describe themselves as members of a particular century and then as part of the legion, suggesting the bonds most important to them. Legions were primarily intended for fighting big battles, but their command structure allowed them to function well as garrisons and administrators for a wide area. Detachments, or vexillations, were frequently employed for duties that did not require a full legion, and these varied in size from several cohorts to a few men.

The Romans had always relied on foreign troops to supplement the numbers of the citizen legions. These included allied troops as well as the followers of tribal war-leaders whose loyalty was to their chief whether he fought with or against Rome. It was particularly common to raise contingents from the area in which the army was campaigning, both because it was easy to do so and also because such troops were usually suited to the conditions of local warfare. Caesar relied largely on Gallic and German cavalry during the conquest of Gaul, but, although effective in battle, these proved poor scouts since reconnaissance played a minor role in tribal warfare. The early Principate saw the creation of the regular *auxilia*, foreign troops uniformed and paid by Rome, and trained to the same standards of discipline as the legions. The men were long-service professional soldiers like the legionaries and served in units that were equally permanent. Unit titles were usually taken from the ethnic group or tribe from which it was first raised. Most *auxilia* served far from their place of origin, and little or no effort was taken to draw new recruits from the original source. Therefore auxiliary units tended to become of mixed nationality, although long service in a province might cause one group to predominate. The language of command and of the unit's administration was always Latin, which made it relatively easy to absorb a mixture of nationalities in a single regiment.

The *auxilia* were never grouped into units of similar size to the legions. The infantry were formed in cohorts and the cavalry in similarly sized *alae*. Each cohort or *ala* was independent, with its own commander, an equestrian usually holding the rank of prefect. A number of auxiliary units were often attached to a legion, and prolonged service together raised the efficiency of such forces, but there was no standard complement of *auxilia* permanently supporting every legion. The smaller size of auxiliary units made it much easier to shift them from one area or province to another. The mixed cohorts (*cohortes equitatae*), which included both foot and horse in a ratio of about four to one, were especially suited to garrison and local policing activities. The *auxilia* provided a more flexible and cheaper supplement to legionary numbers. They also supplied the army with some troop types in which the legions were especially deficient, in particular supplying large numbers of very good quality cavalry. Auxiliary infantry also included units of archers and contingents of slingers, but the traditional view that auxiliary foot were lighter equipped and fought in looser order than the legions is mistaken. The typical auxiliary infantryman wore scale or mail armour of similar weight to the legionary cuirass and a bronze helmet, carried a flat, oval shield and was armed with a *gladius* and a javelin or spear. This is not the equipment of a nimble skirmisher. There may have been a few cohorts with lighter equipment who fought as skirmishers, but we have no direct evidence for this. The vast majority of auxiliary cohorts fought in close order in a way not markedly different from legionaries.

All soldiers enlisted for twenty-five years, the last five of which were spent as a veteran with lighter duties. Auxiliaries were granted Roman citizenship at the end of this period, although sometimes whole units earned this distinction prematurely as a result of distinguished service. The unit kept the title *civium Romanorum* permanently, even when all the men who enjoyed the grant had long since departed. The vast majority of soldiers were volunteers, conscription was rarely imposed except when an allied tribe or kingdom was obliged by treaty to supply a set quota of men for the *auxilia*. The army provided a soldier with a regular if not especially lavish salary paid in hard coin but subject to

Medical orderlies at a field dressing station attend to casualties during a battle in Dacia. The Roman army's medical service was probably more advanced than that of any army until the modern era and many types of wounds could be treated with a good chance of success.

various deductions. His living conditions in barracks were cramped, but then so were those of the urban poor in the Roman world, and soldiers had the advantage of good medical support. His activities were closely regulated and the soldier was subject to a harsh, frequently brutal, and sometimes arbitrary system of discipline. The centurion's vine-cane (*vitis*) was a badge of office, but was frequently used to inflict summary punishment. One centurion, lynched during the mutiny of the Danubian legions in AD 14, was nicknamed 'Bring me another!' (*cedo alteram*) from his habit of beating a soldier's back until his cane snapped and then demanding another. Desertion was always a problem in the professional army, and a frequent motive was the wish to avoid punishment. It was also common practice for centurions and other officers to accept bribes to spare individuals from unpleasant duties. Another aspect of military discipline was the ban on soldiers' marrying, any existing marriage being annulled on enlistment. The main reason for this was a reluctance of the state to accept financial responsibility for soldiers and their families. It is quite clear that many soldiers did live in stable relationships with women and raised children, their families living in the civilian settlements (*canabae*) outside forts or perhaps even inside the barracks. The grant of citizenship to discharged auxiliaries included a clause extending this right to any children, which makes it clear that the ban was not rigidly enforced. The citizen legionaries found it much harder to gain official recognition and citizenship for their children.

The army did offer the prospect of promotion to increasingly senior, more prestigious and better paid ranks, but the high standard of literacy essential for most of these favoured the better-educated recruits. In theory it was possible for an ordinary soldier to advance through the lesser ranks until he became a centurion, progress through the centurionate and hold the rank of *primus pilus*, the senior centurion in a legion, and then be elevated to the equestrian order and be made governor of a minor province or command a cohort of the Praetorian Guard. But such a meteoric rise was highly unlikely, though possible for a family over several generations; more modest advancement was common. As important as talent and education in determining the fortunes of a career was influence. Patronage was all pervasive in Roman society and letters of recommendation are the most common form of literature to survive from antiquity. A letter from an influential friend or family member greatly accelerated a career. On active service any soldier might distinguish himself and so come to the attention of a commander who could promote him, but such opportunities were rare in garrison duty.

Many auxiliaries came from cultures which greatly admired warrior virtues and who found service in the Roman army attractive, but the legions tended to be recruited from the poorest elements of Roman society. As the first century AD progressed, fewer and fewer Italians joined the legions, preferring instead the more lucrative, more comfortable and safer prospect of serving in the Praetorian Guard or other paramilitary forces in Rome itself. Recruits increasingly came from the provinces where there had been a heavy settlement of veteran colonies, and there was also a small but significant number of men born 'in the camp' (*in castris*), the illegitimate sons produced by soldiers' illegal marriages. The rest of society, especially the wealthier classes who feared the army's capacity to plunge the state into civil war, despised soldiers as brutal and greedy. The professional soldiers of the Principate lived in bases on the fringes of the Empire, each surrounded by a civil settlement which provided most of its needs, and after discharge many legionaries settled in colonies with other soldiers. The degree of isolation varied from province to province and in different periods, but it encouraged identification with the soldiers' units. In Polybius' day a soldier decorated for valour returned to Rome and wore his awards during public festivals to the admiration of the rest of society. Now the army formed very much its own community with its own set of distinctly military values. Soldiers were granted status in accordance with their conformity to these standards, and those who were decorated or gained a reputation for martial virtue were respected within the army. Many of the minor distinctions in grade, rank and title which seem to have been important to soldiers may have been as incomprehensible to contemporary civilians as they are to us. Pride in themselves and in their unit was a major factor in making Roman soldiers willing to risk death or appalling injury.

The senior officers of the army were still drawn from the élite of the Roman world and served for comparatively short periods. It has been estimated that a provincial governor, legionary legate, tribune or auxiliary prefect served on average for three years in any post, but there was much variation in this pattern. Greater continuity was provided by the centurions who were career soldiers. Traditionally they have been depicted as the equivalent of NCOs in modern armies, sergeant-majors promoted out of the ranks after long service, who offered the maturity and experience lacking in their 'amateur' senior officers. It is true that we know of a number of individuals who were promoted to the centurionate after service as ordinary soldiers. Equally, we know of a similar number of equestrians who chose to follow a career as legionary centurions and were directly commissioned, and other men who achieved the rank after a period in municipal government. Most centurions seem to have achieved the position after service in some of the junior ranks, perhaps on the staff of the tribune or legate or as one of the *principales* in the century. Patronage is likely to have played a greater part in their selection than ability. Centurions required a very high standard of education and often held positions of considerable responsibility, acting as regional representatives of the civil power in the provinces, or in political or diplomatic roles on the frontiers. They were also men of status, enjoying far higher pay and better conditions than ordinary soldiers. The majority of centurions were probably drawn from the more prosperous and better-educated classes of Roman society whose existence is too often ignored by scholars apt to divide society into 'the aristocratic élite' and 'the poor'.

TRAINING AND TACTICS

'Their battle-drills are no different from the real thing … It would not be far from the truth to call their drills bloodless battles, their battles bloody drills.' Josephus presented an idealized view of the army's efficiency, but while the warriors of many different peoples were well practised in the use of their personal weapons, only the Romans trained both as individuals and units. According to the later military theorist Vegetius, the first thing a new recruit was taught was the military pace: learning how to march in step and keep his place in formation. Personal fitness received a high priority and there were regular route marches of twenty Roman miles in five hours at the normal pace and twenty-four in the same time at the quick step. On some marches the recruits stopped to learn how to lay out and construct a marching camp. They were taught how to use their personal weapons by practising thrusts and cuts against a 1.8-metre post fixed into the ground. At first they used wooden swords and wicker shields of twice the weight of the normal issue to strengthen their arms. On at least one occasion these wooden practice swords were used as batons by troops quelling a riot. After this they fenced with other recruits, the tips of their swords covered with leather pads to prevent serious injury, and finally whole units would fight mock battles. Cavalry practised a complex series of drills involving movement in formation and the throwing of missiles, culminating in the spectacular *Hippaka Gymnasia*, or cavalry games.

Training was not just an experience for recruits but a continual activity to maintain a unit's efficiency. Often the many duties which required the dispersal of a unit hindered its training, but good officers made sure that their men were well drilled and their weapons well maintained. If time permitted at the beginning of a campaign, then most generals exercised their troops to bring them to the peak of efficiency. A monument from the base of Legio III Augusta at Lambaesis in North Africa records a speech made by Hadrian to the army of the province after it had performed several days of exercises. The emperor displayed a detailed knowledge of the units' strength and current deployment as well as a technical understanding of the manoeuvres themselves. He noted that Legio III Augusta had detached one cohort for service with the proconsul of the neighbouring province, had sent a vexillation of another cohort plus four men from each of the other centuries to reinforce another legion, and provided many small detachments to man small outposts and guard stations, while the unit had recently moved its camp twice. These factors might have restricted the ability of the legion to train as a unit, but Hadrian used them to reinforce his praise for their actual performance. Similarly, when addressing the cavalry of a *cohors equitata*, he commented that it was

This first-century cavalry parade helmet from Syria is one of the earliest examples of this type. Such lavishly decorated armour and fittings, combined with brightly coloured clothing and standards added to the spectacle of the cavalry games or Hipparka Gymnasia.

difficult for such a unit to perform satisfactorily immediately after an *ala,* with its larger numbers, better equipment and mounts, had put on a display, before expressing his praise for their achievement. Occasionally Hadrian expressed disapproval of a drill, for instance criticizing a cavalry unit for mounting a charge that was too fast and uncontrolled, but his speech is overwhelmingly one of praise for the units and especially their officers.

Discipline and order were emphasized in all of the army's manoeuvres, whether in training or on campaign. Gone were the days when Roman columns blundered along on the march, risking ambush from a skilful opponent. The army of the Principate moved behind a screen of cavalry outposts, supported by detachments of infantry including a high proportion of missile armed troops. Special units of cavalry known as *exploratores* were formed specifically to perform the role of reconnaissance. If the enemy were close, then the whole army might move in battle formation, each unit in place and ready to deploy from march column into a fighting line. It was common to move with the army formed into a large hollow square if it was uncertain from which direction the enemy might attack. All these techniques had developed gradually during the long experience of frontier warfare, but were perfected in the first century AD. The creation of the regular *auxilia* provided large numbers of well-trained cavalry, who were far better suited to tasks such as scouting than many of the allied contingents, which had served with Republican armies, had ever been.

The greater discipline of the Imperial army was reflected in its battle tactics. In Polybius' day legionaries advanced noisily, banging their weapons against their shields and shouting. From at least Caesar's day, Roman infantry advanced slowly and in silence. Legionaries now carried only one *pilum*. At very short range, probably within 15 metres of the enemy, they threw these in a single volley and charged. Only at this moment did they break the silence and yell their battle cry. In this way they delivered a massive twin-shock to their enemy: the physical shock of a barrage of heavy *pila* and the moral shock of the sudden screaming charge. The noisy advance of the Polybian legion had not been that different to the wild, screaming advance of a Gallic war band. A silent advance was more intimidating and certainly harder to achieve. Only a very high standard of discipline restrained men from releasing their nervous tension by instinctively yelling and running forward to get the impending clash over with, a tendency which broke up their formation. A slower, steadier advance kept the ranks in order, allowed the officers to keep control over the formation and ensured that the unit remained a dense mass throughout the charge. Such an advance appeared unstoppable and there was a good chance that the enemy would be broken before the charge went home, or after a very brief burst of fighting. If this did not happen then the resulting combat was much the same as one fought by a manipular legion. Roman doctrine emphasized individual aggression, and soldiers were taught to get close to their opponent in order to use their short-bladed *gladii*. The standard drill was to punch the enemy in the face with the shield-boss and then stab him in the stomach. In an ideal situation his opponent had already lost his shield to a thrown *pilum*. The Roman *scutum* was very heavy: weights of reconstructions have ranged from 5.5 to 10 kilograms (12–22 lbs), and a blow delivered with the weight of the body behind the soldier's left hand stood a good chance of overbalancing an opponent. This might not always be possible and Roman soldiers were trained to deliver a wide range of cuts and thrusts. Crouched behind a *scutum*, most of the soldier's torso was

The Roman army in Lower Moesia recorded its role in the Dacian Wars in several monuments at Adamklissi in modern-day Romania, including these reliefs or Metopes from the Troepaeum Traiani. More crudely carved than Trajan's Column, they give a far more accurate view of the equipment actually worn on campaign. This legionary soldier wears mail, instead of the segmented armour, has extra armour on his right arm and greaves strapped to his calves. He is punching his enemy in the face with his shield boss and then stabbing him in the stomach with his sword, a clear artistic representation of the classic Roman fighting technique described by our literary sources.

well protected and the design of the helmet and all types of cuirass gave extra protection to the head and shoulders, vulnerable to downward cuts. However, Roman infantry helmets left the face and ears uncovered to allow men to hear orders and see clearly what was going on around them, so that wounds to the face were common. The junior leaders of the Roman army, especially the centurions, led aggressively, and individual boldness by all ranks was encouraged by the lavish reward, decoration and promotion granted to those who distinguished themselves. Discipline and unit pride gave the Romans great staying power in combat, keeping them in close contact with the enemy, but victories were won by the few men who were prepared to go first and cut a path into the enemy ranks. Roman generals kept close to the fighting so that they were able to reward such men. They

This Metope shows three Roman standard bearers, two vexilla *or flags flanking a wreathed standard, probably originally topped by an eagle. Standards were physical expressions of a unit's corporate identity and were treated with great reverence. In a permanent camp they were kept in a special shrine in the unit's headquarters or* principia. *All soldiers at Adamklissi are depicted as clean shaven, unlike the legionaries on Trajan's Column, many of whom have thick beards. This scene, like many others at Adamklissi, has a nearly identical companion, possibly to represent the two legions garrisoning Lower Moesia.*

were also in a good position to gauge how the combat was going and commit or lead in reserve cohorts accordingly.

The legionary cohort was very much a functional tactical unit and was rarely a focus of especially strong loyalty. The cohort was almost certainly commanded by the *pilus prior*, its senior centurion, although no contemporary source explicitly states this. There were few tactical options available to the commander of a cohort, and his main job was to move the men under his command as a body to wherever they were required to be. He then needed to control the cohort's advance, ensuring that the volley of *pila* and final running charge were delivered on order and did not come as a spontaneous outburst. Once in close contact with the enemy, then much responsibility devolved on to the other centurions and the *principales* in each century. Their job was to inspire the men, to organize and lead as many as possible in successive rushes forward until the enemy had been routed. After that the senior centurion once again needed to regain control over the whole cohort, to restore order and prepare his tired men to move and perhaps fight again as a unit. In a large battle there was relatively little scope for independent action at the cohort level, and the centurions commanding them formed part of a command structure which allowed the legionary legate to control the five thousand men under his command more easily, and indirectly enabled the commander-in-chief to direct his whole force. In a large battle most auxiliary cohorts acted to all intents and purposes like the identically sized legionary cohorts. However, their lack of a clear command structure above the level of the cohort made them harder to manoeuvre in large numbers, and less easy to employ as reserves. Auxiliaries were often deployed as the army's first line, allowing the more easily controlled legionaries to act as supports; alternatively they might be spread out on the army's flanks.

Roman infantry doctrine stressed that it was always wise to advance to meet enemy infantry, since a charge encouraged aggression, whereas passively waiting to receive a charge was dispiriting. A sudden infantry charge could rout disordered or stationary cavalry, stampeding the horses, but it was normally wise for foot to meet cavalry at the halt. A cavalry charge was an immensely intimidating sight. Scattered or dispersed infantry were helpless against it, since most men would flee and allow the horsemen to cut down with ease even those who attempted to fight. Arrian describes a formation designed to resist a charge by the heavily armoured horsemen of the Alans. The legionaries were formed eight ranks deep, the first four armed with the *pilum*, the remainder with a lighter javelin, probably the *lancea*. The front rank held their *pila* at forty-five degrees, the butts braced against the ground so that they presented a dense row of points to the enemy. The men in the next three ranks, after throwing their *pila*, braced themselves against the men in front. The remaining legionaries threw their *lanceae* while a ninth rank of foot-archers, a tenth rank of horse-archers, and artillery added to the barrage of missiles. This heavy weight of missiles would have brought

The pride of the Roman cavalry were the horsemen of the alae, *but more numerous were the soldiers of the mixed infantry and cavalry* cohortes equitatae. *These men were not as highly paid, or as well mounted as the men of the* alae, *but they performed much of the army's day-to-day patrolling and escort duties.*

down a fair number of cavalrymen, but even those who survived would not have been able to get into contact with the infantry since their horses would instinctively refuse to gallop into such a seemingly solid object. Once the charge was stopped the continual deluge of javelins and arrows continued to weaken them as they stood impotently a few metres from the infantry line, until they were inevitably forced to withdraw. Such a solid formation deterred the cavalry from approaching by its very appearance, while the densely packed ranks prevented the Romans from running away. Such a formation was only possible with stationary troops, especially since Arrian advocated a solid infantry line with none of the usual intervals between the cohorts.

Cavalry were unable to hold ground and combats between horse were very fluid, fast-moving affairs, in which successful charges spent their momentum in pursuit, the horses becoming blown and vulnerable to fresh enemy reserves. The Romans were careful always to leave at least half of their available cavalry in separate supporting lines behind the main advance. Horses will refuse to charge straight into an oncoming line of cavalry, so when combats occurred it was because either the two lines had opened their files, allowing them to gallop through each other's formation, or they had halted just before contact, at which point individuals would begin to walk their mounts forward to get within sword's or spear's reach of the enemy. In the latter case the mêlée was likely to be longer and more bloody than the former. More often than not one side or the other turned and fled before the chargers came into contact. Selected infantry were often deployed in close support of cavalry, sometimes travelling to battle by running alongside the horsemen and clinging to the horses' manes. Such infantry rarely intermingled within the ranks of a cavalry formation. Instead, they formed dense knots of infantry behind the main cavalry line. When a friendly cavalry unit was forced to retreat it could shelter and re-form behind one of these infantry blocks, the infantry driving off any pursuers with missiles.

ROME AND PARTHIA

For nearly three centuries after their first clash in 54 BC, the Parthians were the most dangerous opponents the Romans faced in the eastern part of the Empire. The Parthian military system and philosophy was radically different from the Roman and their army relied almost exclusively on cavalry. There were Parthian infantry, most of whom were said to have been archers, but they were of poor quality and receive very little mention in our sources. The strength of the Parthian army lay in its two types of cavalry, the heavily armoured cataphracts and the light horse-archers. It was the latter who most encapsulated the Parthian military philosophy. Horse-archers were unarmoured and would stage a mounted charge only as a last resort against an enemy who was already weakened. Instead, they used their powerful composite bows to shoot down their enemies and the mobility of their swift horses to avoid contact and make themselves difficult targets for return fire. Firing from a moving horse did not make for accurate shooting, but the objective was to pepper the target area with as many arrows as possible so that some were bound to find a mark. Only when the enemy had been weakened by this constant barrage would the cataphracts charge and break them. If the enemy's strength and determination seemed undiminished then the Parthians withdrew and continued to shadow their opponents, waiting for a more favourable opportunity. The Parthians would certainly flee if the situation was unfavourable. The readiness with which the Parthians fled but then rounded on any incautious pursuers always astonished the Romans. It made it very difficult to inflict a decisive defeat on them in battle since it was so easy for the enemy horsemen to escape. In 36 BC Mark Antony's soldiers were dismayed to discover that a Parthian rout and vigorous Roman pursuit produced only thirty dead and eighty prisoners.

When the Romans and Parthians first encountered each other in battle at Carrhae in 53 BC, both sides were overconfident. The Romans had grown used to brushing aside the armies of Armenia and Pontus with consummate ease. The greater part of the Roman cavalry and light infantry rashly pursued a Parthian withdrawal, became separated from the main force, were surrounded and annihilated. Throughout the rest of the day the square formed by the legions came under a heavy barrage of arrows, the Parthians regularly replenishing their quivers from a well-organized supply of ammunition carried by the camel train. Many Romans were wounded, but the army was never weakened to the point where it could be swept aside by a cataphract charge, and the situation reached something of a stalemate. However, the Roman army and its commander lost heart and decided to withdraw, abandoning its wounded. The Parthians, ideally suited to harassing a retreating foe, especially one that was mostly on foot, pursued with vigour and nearly all of the Roman army was slaughtered or forced to surrender, the legions losing their precious eagles. This complete success encouraged the Parthians to despise Roman armies, especially since the force at Carrhae represented only part of their strength and had been expected to

This terracotta statuette shows a galloping Parthian horse-archer about to fire his recurved composite bow. Later Arabic manuals advised that the archer should aim to loose his arrow when his horse was in mid stride. Accuracy was to be sacrificed to deluge the target with as many missiles as possible, before the archer withdrew out of range of any return fire.

delay and not to defeat the enemy. Their attempted invasion of Syria ended in disaster, however, when on two occasions Parthian armies dashed themselves to pieces attacking uphill against confident legionaries supported by slingers, whose missiles might give a cataphract concussion even if they did not penetrate his armour. After this both sides treated the opponent with caution and Roman armies marching against the Parthians made sure that they included a good proportion of cavalry and infantry armed with missile weapons. Even more importantly they used all elements of the army to support each other, the heavy infantry to provide solidity, the archers and slingers to keep the enemy at a distance – bowmen on foot will usually outrange horse-archers – and the cavalry to mount carefully controlled counter-attacks. The Parthians, true to their military doctrine, would refuse to join battle with such a well-prepared force, although they would attempt to lure out and isolate for destruction any small detachments whose commanders were over bold. Skilful Roman generals kept their subordinates under tightly control when campaigning against the Parthians.

The result was a stand off. The Romans could not force the mobile Parthians into a decisive battle and the Parthians could not prevent a well-prepared and well-handled Roman army from marching through their territory. The Romans targeted Parthian cities and strongholds, besieging and storming them one by one. The Parthian capital, Ctesiphon, was sacked several times. The Parthians exploited their mobility to attack the Romans' supply lines, or distract their attention by deep raids into Syria or the kingdoms allied to Rome. Antony's invasion failed when his siege-train, lagging behind the main columns and protected by two legions, was captured in its entirety. In the resultant retreat he was harassed by the Parthians and suffered enormous losses, mostly from disease and shortage of provisions. A war fought under Nero went very well for the Romans, until one poorly led army suffered a reverse, was jostled into a panicked flight and surrendered, the legionaries undergoing the humiliation of being sent under the yoke. An invasion of Parthia was a massive undertaking requiring huge numbers of troops to make the advancing armies strong enough both to deter Parthian attacks and to be able to besiege and take their cities. In addition, more soldiers were needed to protect the lines of communication that supplied the advancing forces and to defend Rome's provinces again Parthian attacks. All these troops needed to be fed and supplied, and much of the campaigning area was not productive enough to allow the troops to support themselves by foraging, an activity which anyway left small detachments isolated and vulnerable to the mobile enemy. The size of Parthia and the time-consuming task of taking strongholds one by one until the Parthian king was forced to come to terms made an invasion an undertaking of several years. Only the emperor himself could command such an enterprise, without the probability of creating a dangerous rival, and few felt inclined to spend long years on campaign in the east. Ultimately, the scale of the task and the difficulty of finding sufficient manpower prevented a Roman conquest of Parthia, and conflicts came instead to focus on domination of the kingdoms between the two empires, notably Armenia.

The Romans initiated most of the conflicts with Parthia, save when, in AD 155, the Parthian king launched an unprovoked invasion of Armenia and followed on to attack Syria. The Parthians' lack of skill in siege warfare meant that their invasions tended to consist of large-scale raids. Parthia was always very weak internally and rarely presented a real threat to the stability of the Roman east. Theoretically the Arsacid king controlled sufficient wealth from the prosperous Hellenistic cities and the profits of the major trade routes to maintain his dominance over the aristocracy. In practice the great noble families had usurped many royal prerogatives and provided the majority of troops for the royal army, supplied in contingents on a feudal basis. In many ways it was not in the interest of the monarch for the military followers of noblemen to be too effective. Surenas, the successful commander at Carrhae, was executed because the king feared him as a potential rival. Therefore the political system prevented the army from becoming too effective. The continual renewal of war with the Parthians has been interpreted as an indication that Roman imperialism had not died with the Republic, and that the dream of world conquest and the desire to emulate Alexander the Great still motivated many emperors. The underlying cause of this hostility is simpler and was due to the Roman understanding of war which we have already discussed. The Parthians had fought and humiliated the Romans and were therefore enemies. Until they ceased to be perceived in this way by being absorbed as subordinate allies or conquered as a province, then renewal of hostilities was inevitable.

PAX ROMANA

Soldiers were present in small numbers throughout the Empire. The army was often called upon to perform a great range of duties that had little to do with its military role, largely because the Empire lacked a sizeable 'civil service'. Soldiers appear supervising building work, assisting state officials in such tasks as tax collecting, guarding city prisons, regulating traffic through cities, or acting as policemen. In the New Testament we find a centurion commanding the detachment which carried out the crucifixion of Christ, and two others: the centurion sent to take the Apostle Paul to Rome, and in Galilee a centurion who had supervised the construction of a synagogue, although the last man may well have been from the army of the Herods, organized on the Roman model and later absorbed into the *auxilia*. As these passages suggest, centurions in particular were often encountered as representatives of Roman authority at a local level. Records on papyrus include appeals to centurions for protection against domestic violence and robbery, and for them to investigate murders and disappearances. Other small parties of soldiers were scattered to supply the army's needs, manufacturing or collecting equipment, forage or animals, quarrying for stone, and recruiting. There are very many records of complaints against soldiers, accusations of brutal treatment of civilians and illegal seizure of property, often under the guise of requisitioning. Soldiers, especially detached from their unit and away from authority, certainly seem to have been guilty of abusing their power over civilians, but our sources are more likely to mention the cases of friction than of peaceful interaction, and it is difficult to estimate the nature of the majority of relations between the army and civilian population.

Many legions, or large *vexillationes*, were positioned in or near the great cities of the eastern empire. The greater part of the two legions forming the garrison of Egypt were based near Alexandria with the clear intention of over-awing this great political centre. The army was frequently called in to quell rioting in the city. This deployment has led to the suggestion that the Roman army, at least in some provinces, was primarily an army of occupation whose main role was to control the subject population. The depiction of the Roman army as a brutal oppressor is an attractive one for a generation of scholars who view empires as inherently wrong. When the army was called in to punish communities for failing to pay taxes or flouting the authority of the governor's representatives, it proved brutally efficient at burning villages and crucifying large numbers to terrify the rest into submission. Such action was relatively rare and it is important to remember that the army did not number more than 250–300,000 at this period, compared to the population of the Empire roughly estimated at 70 million. The Roman army was not large enough to have ruled purely through naked force, and much of the population of the provinces benefited from the existence of the Empire. The wealthiest gained Roman citizenship, became equestrians or senators and might follow the military careers open to these classes, while local aristocrats provided many centurions for the *auxilia*.

Nor were all the outbreaks of violence within the Empire due to hatred of Roman rule. One of the most frequent causes of rioting in Alexandria was tension between the Jewish and Gentile communities there, and fighting between the Samaritans and Jews in Judaea was also common. Rivalry among neighbouring cities, or political factions within a city, occasionally spilt over into rioting and disturbances. Banditry was rife in some areas, especially at times of economic hardship, but, even when this was in part motivated by hatred of Rome, the targets were

THE SIEGE OF JERUSALEM AD 70

In AD 66 the main outbreak of the Jewish rebellion occurred at Jerusalem and received further encouragement when a hastily raised Roman army commanded by the Syrian governor, Cestius Gallus, marched against the city only to suffer heavy losses and retreat in disorder. The rebels were never united under a single leader, but were divided into various factions and often fought amongst themselves. By 70 nearly all of the rebel strongholds had been taken by the Romans and only Jerusalem remained as the heart of the resistance. Three leaders dominated different parts of the city and the bitter fighting between their followers was only ended when Titus and the Roman army arrived outside the city walls. As in most sieges in this period, much fighting occurred outside the fortifications. It was a sign of the defender's confidence that he was willing to contest the ground outside the walls, forcing the attackers to fight to control the ground approaching the walls, a necessary preliminary to any siegeworks. The Romans were surprised by the active nature of the Jewish defence of Jerusalem. Throughout the siege the defenders continually sallied out to attack the Roman camps and siegeworks.

(1) The Romans attack the Third Wall, making a breach after fifteen days despite fierce resistance. The Jewish rebels abandon this part of the city, allowing the Romans to occupy it without fighting

(2) The Romans camp inside the Third Wall, demolishing the houses over a wide area. The defenders make frequent sallies and heavy fighting ensues. The Romans breach the Second Wall, but their attacking columns are defeated after an initial success. The wall falls permanently four days later

(3) Titus orders four siege ramps to be constructed. Completed after seventeen days, these are immediately destroyed by the rebels. Titus orders the construction of the line of circumvallation. Two new ramps are then built against the Fortress of Antonia. The defenders' countermining undermines their fortifications which collapse

(4) The Romans are now able to attack the Great Temple. Several assaults fail in weeks of heavy fighting. Eventually the Romans break in and the Temple is burnt down. This defeat takes the heart out of the defenders

(5) The Romans launch attacks from the Temple into the Old City. After eighteen days of preparation they storm the area around the former palace of Herod the Great. The rebels put up little resistance and the siege is over

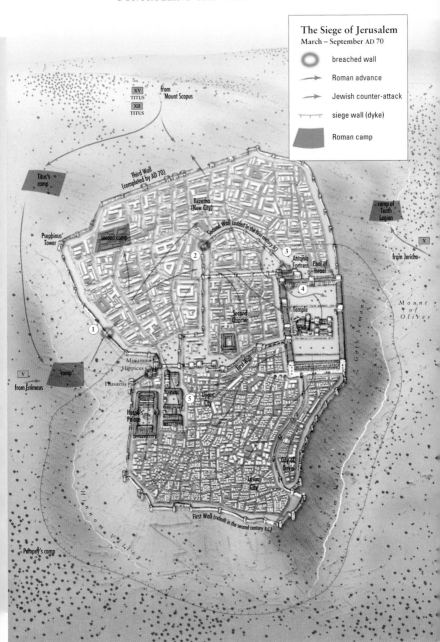

The Siege of Jerusalem
March – September AD 70

breached wall

Roman advance

Jewish counter-attack

siege wall (dyke)

Roman camp

XV
TITUS

XII
TITUS

from
Mount Scopus

Titus's
camp

Third Wall
(completed by AD 70)

Bezetha
(New City)

Second Wall (added in the first century AD)

camp of
Tenth
Legion

X

Psephinus'
Tower

second camp

Antonia
Fortress

Pool of
Israel

from Jericho

Mount
of
Olives

Second
Quarter

Temple

First Wall

Miriamne
Hippicus

Phasaelis

camp

V

from Emmaus

Upper
City

Herod's
Palace

City of
David

Lower
City

Hinnom Valley

Kidron Valley

Gethsemane

First Wall (rebuilt in the second century B.C.)

Pompey's camp

This relief from the Arch of Titus shows the spoils carried in his triumph celebrating the capture of Jerusalem. Titus had assumed command of the army in Judaea after Vespasian declared himself a candidate for the throne. His exploits are described with a great degree of sycophancy by the historian Josephus.

more often than not an area's civilian population. It is impossible to tell at this distance in time whether rebels or bandits were able to find refuge within civilian communities because of general sympathy for their cause or fear of their violence. Unrest in many areas was not a creation of Roman rule, but inherited from previous kingdoms and empires or the result of ethnic tension. Its chief motivation was more often social and economic rather than political.

Rebellions that were intended to throw off Roman rule did occur, most often within a generation of an area's conquest, as in Germany, Gaul and Britain. If this outbreak was defeated, then most areas steadily became absorbed into the imperial culture, their aristocracies profiting from association with the new power. Perhaps the most continuous resistance to Roman rule was found in Judaea, where sporadic uprisings and banditry exploded into massed rebellion in 66–74 and 133–5. A wider rebellion of Jewish communities in Egypt, Libya and Cyprus caused great turmoil under Trajan (115–17). The Jews were exceptional among the peoples of the Roman east in having a strong sense of national identity and culture which reached back far beyond the Greek and Roman presence in the area. Religion emphasized their distinctiveness and prevented the aristocracy from adopting careers in imperial service.

When an uprising did occur, the Roman reaction was always the same. All the troops which could be mustered at short notice were formed into a column and sent immediately to confront the perceived centre of the rebellion. It took a great number of vehicles, draught and baggage animals to supply an army for a long campaign. The Roman army did not maintain such a large baggage train on a permanent basis, but requisitioned the transport required once a war threatened, a process requiring time. This often meant that numerically small and poorly supplied Roman columns launched an immediate offensive against the rebels. Ideally, a show of force, even if it was a façade, regained the initiative and prevented a rebellion from developing and growing stronger. The willingness of even greatly outnumbered Roman forces to attack the enemy displayed a contempt for them and an unwavering belief in the Romans' inevitable victory. It was a gamble since the Roman column was only capable of defeating relatively weak opposition and risked disaster if it encountered a well-prepared and strong enemy. Both Boudicca in AD 60 and the Jewish rebels in 66 received a great boost when they won victories over the first, poorly prepared Roman forces sent against them. If the Romans failed to crush the rebellion in its early stages, then the next army sent against the rising was properly prepared to fight a major war.

One great advantage enjoyed by the Roman army was its skill in siege warfare. Both the rebellion of 66–74 and the Bar Kochba revolt were dominated by sieges as the Romans systematically stormed the Jewish strongholds. Most of the technology of siege warfare had been developed in the Hellenistic world when its secrets had been the preserve of a relatively small group of professional engineers, often serving as mercenaries. Battering-rams breached the enemy defences, artillery firing bolts and stones suppressed the defenders, and siege towers made it easier for the attacking parties to reach the walls. The legions of the Principate had men well trained in constructing and operating all of these engines as part of their standard complement, as well as artillery and other equipment, much of it prefabricated for easier transportation. The Romans did relatively little to develop the technical side of siegecraft, but they brought an aggressive, relentless

The fortress of Masada was built near the Dead Sea by Herod the Great as a luxurious place of refuge in an apparently impregnable position. In AD 73 when Legio X Fretensis besieged the fortress it was held by Jewish extremists known as the Sicarii. Deep cisterns and vast storerooms held an almost inexhaustible supply of food and water, so the Romans decided on a direct assault, building a huge ramp against the western side of the hill. Faced with defeat, the Sicarii committed suicide after murdering their families.

quality to this type of warfare. Earlier Roman armies had been forced to blockade a fortress and starve the defenders into submission if it had not fallen to an immediate surprise attack. Now they undertook massive labour, constructing ramps to bring their rams and towers against the defences. Once a breach had been created, infantry, supported by artillery fire, were sent into the assault. Such attacks were always difficult and the storming party suffered heavy casualties. A successful assault left the attackers out of control; the resulting sack of a city was an appalling thing, with the men being massacred and the women raped and enslaved. Roman law denied any rights to defenders who failed to surrender before the first ram touched their wall, and the horrific consequences of a Roman assault were intended to encourage an early surrender. Throughout the siege, the Romans took every opportunity to terrorize the defenders, captives taken during sallies being crucified in sight of the walls or their severed heads fired by artillery into the city. It was common for the Romans to build a ditch and wall, or line of circumvallation, around the entire stronghold, preventing anyone from escaping or supplies and reinforcements from reaching the defenders. It also served as a reminder that while the defenders may have fenced themselves in for their own protection, the Romans had now fenced them in for their ultimate destruction.

THE FRONTIERS

The greater part of the Roman army, especially in the western provinces, was based in the frontier zones. There has been considerable debate over the role of the army in these areas, and indeed of the Roman concept of frontiers, but it is very important to note that the Empire's frontiers did not represent clear geographical limits to the army's activity. The Romans were heavily involved both diplomatically and militarily for a considerable distance beyond the boundaries of the provinces. Centurions attended tribal meetings of many of the peoples of north-west Europe. Noblemen thought to be favourable to the Romans were paid large subsidies, allowing them to support a bigger band of followers and increase their status within the tribe. Ideally, this deterred the tribes from large-scale aggression, and at the very least it gave the Romans advance warning of its likelihood. Warfare and especially raiding played a central role in the society of many of the peoples outside the frontiers in Britain, Germany and along the

Danube. Status within a tribe came from success in war, and attacks against the Roman Empire brought tremendous prestige as well as the prospect of considerable loot. Our sources usually only mention the very large raids by thousands of warriors which penetrated deep into the peaceful provinces. Most barbarian military activity was on a smaller scale; a nobleman and his immediate retainers plus as many other warriors as were attracted by his prestige, probably no more than a few hundred men in total. Some incursions may have been even smaller. There did not need to be any specific motive for such attacks, any more than there needed to be a motive for the constant intertribal raiding. Tacitus claimed that German tribes liked to maintain a depopulated area around their territory to deter enemies by this

The Roman Empire
AD 214

- Roman Empire
- Client state
- disputed territory in northern Britain
- Legionary bases in AD 214
- frontier of the Roman Empire

THE ROMAN EMPIRE IN AD 214

The Roman Empire reached its fullest extent under the Severans. The vast majority of units continued to be stationed in the frontier provinces, with the exception of the Syrian and Egyptian legions who covered the great cities of the east. There was also now a legion permanently stationed outside Rome which, with the addition of the Guard units, provided the Emperor with the basis of a powerful army.

symbol of prowess and to give more warning of approaching raiders. In themselves such small-scale incursions did not threaten the stability of the Empire, but the danger if they went unchecked was that a perception of Roman vulnerability would encourage an escalation in the size and number of attacks.

The number of Roman troops was very small in relation to the size of most of the frontier areas which they occupied. The army lacked the capacity to intercept every raid. One solution might have been to conquer and incorporate the hostile tribes into the Empire. Domitian sought to control the Chatti by advancing the frontier and building a line of forts in their territory. However, conquest required large numbers of troops, most of which would then be tied down as garrisons, and anyway expansion under the Empire needed to be carefully supervised by the emperor. Ideally, diplomatic activity reduced the hostility of the tribes, but often this had to be combined with military force. If the Romans could not stop the raids then they could ensure that the tribes responsible did not go unpunished. Fast-moving columns of troops, stripped of unnecessary baggage and carrying only enough supplies for the duration of the expedition, launched sudden attacks on the tribes, burning their settlements, destroying their crops and rounding up livestock. Only a small area would feel the actual effects of such a punitive expedition, but it demonstrated that the Romans could and would punish attacks upon them with appalling ferocity. Mustering a tribal army took time, and if one did muster to confront the Romans it was usually only when they were withdrawing. A competently handled Roman force could expect to overcome significantly larger tribal armies, so that often a defeat in battle was added to punishment inflicted.

In a sense the Romans had joined in the traditional patterns of intertribal warfare, with the distinction that their attacks were on a more massive scale. With their better organization and logistic support the Romans were also able to attack at any time of the year, usually with the benefit of surprise. The flexibility of the Roman military

More common than unbroken boundaries such as ditches or walls were systems of small outposts, like this watchtower on the River Danube depicted on Trajan's Column. These were used to pass signals, hence the wooden pyre and piles of straw ready to be ignited. Other similar installations were built along the line of road systems policed by the army, for instance in Egypt.

system allowed them to adapt to fighting different cultures. If a people possessed a strong field army and a willingness to fight open battles, then the defeat of this force usually ensured their surrender. If they possessed important political and economic centres, such as cities, then these were besieged and captured. A people who refused battle or lacked large, important settlements faced attacks on their villages, their cattle and crops. One of the most important symbols of wealth in Germanic society was cattle, making their capture a valuable way of applying pressure on tribal leaders. The Romans were aware of the respect accorded to noblewomen in German society, and as a result demanded these as hostages. Punitive raids were at best temporary solutions to the problem, lasting only as long as the fear they created, while the memory of burning villages ensured a legacy of hatred so that each new generation added the Romans to the list of a tribe's enemies. The Romans needed to maintain an appearance of overwhelming power, since any perception of weakness, such as the reduction in size of a frontier garrison or, even worse, the smallest Roman defeat, risked a return to general hostility.

Roman frontier zones were always based on good communications, usually by road, but also along rivers such as the Rhine and Danube. Bases were established along the line of these routes, allowing swift concentration of forces. Auxiliary forts accommodating single cohorts or *alae* were located further forward, with the great legionary fortresses some distance to the rear. By the end of the first century most of the early turf and timber forts constructed by the Romans were being replaced by more permanent stone structures. The garrisons of these forts were not static and it is now clear that detachments of legionaries and auxiliaries were freely mixed in the forward areas. Often little more than a unit's records and administrative HQ were permanently in residence at their base and the bulk of the unit might be far afield. In the late first and early second century the concept of a line of bases linked by a road was taken a stage further and linear barriers were constructed. The most famous example is Hadrian's Wall running across northern Britain between the Tyne and Solway, but other linear systems were constructed in North Africa, and covered the gap between the Rivers Rhine and Danube. Most of these structures were relatively simple combinations of ditches, ramparts and palisade walls linking together small outpost fortlets and watchtowers. On Hadrian's Wall there were small fortlets, or milecastles, every Roman mile, and two small turrets in between. Most of these walls were not topped by walkways and it is not even certain if this was the case with Hadrian's Wall. In some areas lines of small watchtowers were built without the connecting wall. These great fortified lines are barely mentioned, let alone explained, in our literary sources. Our understanding of them is based almost exclusively on their archaeological remains and it is not always possible to deduce their exact function. What is obvious is that these were not fighting platforms from which the Romans fought off the barbarian hordes who recklessly hurled themselves against the bastions of civilization. Hadrian's Wall from its first inception included

THE FRONTIERS IN NORTHERN BRITAIN

*Archaeological records tell us that a line of forts running along a road known now
as the Stanegate was replaced by a solid wall under Hadrian. This was later replaced
by the more northern Antonine Wall, which was itself abandoned and re-occupied
before the army finally returned to Hadrian's Wall.*

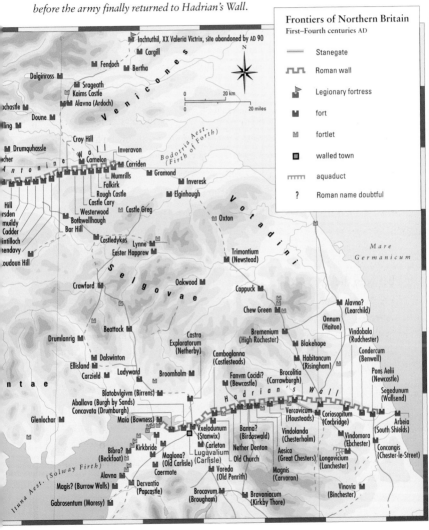

Frontiers of Northern Britain
First–Fourth centuries AD

——	Stanegate
ᴨᴨᴨ	Roman wall
⚑	Legionary fortress
⬛	fort
⬚	fortlet
▣	walled town
ᴨᴨᴨ	aquaduct
?	Roman name doubtful

Inchtuthil, XX Valeria Victrix, site abandoned by AD 90
Cargill
Fendoch   Bertha
Dalginross
Srageath
Kaims Castle
ochastle   Alavna (Ardoch)
Doune
lling
Drumquhassle
cher   Croy Hill   Inveravon
A n t o n i n e   W a l l   Camelon   Carriden
Mumrills   Gramond
Falkirk   Inveresk
Rough Castle   Elginhaugh
Hill   Castle Cary   Castle Greg
rsden   Westerwood
muildy   Bothwellhaugh   Oxton
Cadder   Bar Hill
intilloch   Castledykes
nendavy   Lynne
oudoun Hill   Easter Happrew   Trimontium
(Newstead)
Crawford   Oakwood
Cappuck
Beattock   Chew Green   Alavna?
(Learchild)
Drumlanrig   Castra   Bremenium   Onnum
Exploratorum   (High Rochester)   (Haiton)   Vindobala
(Netherby)   Blakehope   (Rudchester)
Ellisland   Dalswinton   Camboglanna   Habitancum   Condercum
Carzield   Ladyward   (Castlesteads)   (Risingham)   (Benwell)
Broomholm   Fanvm Cocidi?   Brocolitia   Pons Aelii
ntae   (Bewcastle)   (Carrawburgh)   (Newcastle)
Blatobvlgivm (Birrens)   Segedunum
Aballava (Burgh by Sands)   H a d r i a n ' s   W a l l   (Wallsend)
Concavata (Drumburgh)   Vercovicum   Coriosopitum
Glenlochar   Maia (Bowness)   (Houseteads)   (Corbridge)   Arbeia
Vxelodunum   Banna?   Vindolanda   Vindomora   (South Shields)
Bibra?   Kirkbride   (Stanwix)   (Birdoswald)   (Chesterholm)   (Ebchester)   Concangis
(Beckfoot)   Carleton   Nether Denton   Aesica   Longovicium   (Chester-le-Street)
Maglona?   Lugvvalium   Old Church   (Great Chesters)   (Lanchester)
Alavna   (Old Carlisle)   (Carlisle)   Voreda   Magnis
Magis? (Burrow Walls)   Caermote   (Old Penrith)   (Carvoran)   Vinovia
Derventio   Brocavum   (Binchester)
Gabrosentum (Moresy)   (Papcastle)   (Brougham)   Bravoniacum
(Kirkby Thore)

Venicones
Votadini
Selgovae
Bodotria Aest.
(Firth of Forth)
Mare
Germanicum
Itvna Aest. (Solway Firth)

N
0   20 km
0   20 miles

Hadrian's Wall crossing Cawfield Crags in Northumbria. Initially the western section was built of turf and timber, but this was later replaced with stone. To the south the military zone was marked by a wide ditch. Later forts were added to the line of the wall, in some cases, as at Housesteads, being built over earlier turrets. The wall allowed the army to control all traffic passing through the region, which could only cross it at guarded gateways. It was also visually very impressive. We cannot be certain of its original height, nor whether it possessed a continuous walkway allowing sentries to pace along its length.

gateways and crossing points at every milecastle, and when initial plans were modified and forts were constructed on the line of the wall itself, then these added to the number of gateways. Hadrian's Wall was never intended to restrict the movements of the Roman army, but simply provided a secure base for its advance. The Romans maintained permanent outposts beyond the line of the wall and major problems were dealt with by mobile operations even further afield. It did allow the Romans to control movement through the area, since all crossing points were guarded. We know that there were restrictions placed on German tribesmen crossing the Rhine and especially on their carrying of weapons. In this way it did much to prevent the small-scale raiding which formed the bulk of military activity on the frontiers. Preventing many of these incursions discouraged an escalation of hostility into larger-scale warfare. Linear boundaries were only feasible in certain geographical conditions, but small outposts and watchtowers served much the same purpose, creating the impression that a wide area was under continuous surveillance and thus helping to deter raiders. It is also worth bearing in mind the physical impression created by these structures. A fortification running from one horizon to the other was a powerful statement of Rome's might. Caesar tells us that some Gallic tribes cultivated thick hedge lines marking the borders of their territory to deter raiders. In many areas the Romans took care to maintain an area bare of settlement for some distance in advance of the frontier. Whether the Romans intended this or not, it is likely that their frontier systems were perceived as clear demarcations of territory by many barbarian tribes. This reinforces the idea that the Romans had joined in, albeit as a massively stronger participant, the traditional pattern of intertribal warfare.

The Roman army of the Principate was a relatively small but high quality force most suited to mobile operations. Its military doctrine remained intensely aggressive even though the pace of conquest had been drastically reduced and it was increasingly deployed in semi-permanent frontier zones. Measures were taken to police small-scale banditry, raiding and violence both on the frontiers and within the provinces, but the reaction to any major opposition was to assume an immediate offensive. Whatever the local situation, the Roman army adapted its doctrine, deployment and tactics to make the most of the advantages it enjoyed over its less organized and skilled opponents. The frontiers were not static defences, but bases for military and diplomatic activity reaching far beyond the provinces. The Roman military system was flexible enough to adapt to local requirements, but still retained the distinctively relentless pursuit of final victory.

CHAPTER FIVE

Crisis and Reform

Captive barbarians implore the mercy of
Emperor Marcus Aurelius. An intellectual,
who corresponded with the great
philosophical schools in Athens and wrote
his own Meditations, Marcus Aurelius
spent much of his reign campaigning
against the Germanic tribes beyond the
Danube. He planned to add extensive new
provinces in the area of Bohemia, but the
project was abandoned on his death.

Crisis and Reform

THE MIDDLE OF THE third century witnessed frequent Roman defeats. Germanic tribesmen raided deep into the western provinces of the Empire, while most of the east was overrun by the Sassanid Persians. In 251 the emperor Decius was killed when his army was defeated by the Goths. In 260 the emperor Valerian and his army surrendered to the Persians. A short-lived independent empire in Gaul and another in the East based around the kingdom of Palmyra threatened to fragment the Empire. Endemic civil wars sapped the army's strength and weakened its capacity to fight foreign wars. Some stability was achieved under strong emperors such as Aurelian, Diocletian and Constantine, but only after the army's structure and deployment had been greatly altered. Nevertheless, by the early fifth century most of the factors which would lead to the collapse of the western empire were already in place. The reasons for Rome's fall are both complex and fiercely debated, and a full discussion of these would be out of place here, but it is important to consider whether military weakness and inefficiency played a major role in this process. Did the Roman army evolve to deal more effectively with a changed situation, or was it simply in decline?

CIVIL WARS AND USURPATIONS

It is tempting to view civil conflicts as aberrations, campaigns which distracted the army from its primary role of defending the Empire, but which did not have a profound effect on its structure and deployment. However, civil war was a common occurrence in the later Empire and accounted for the greater number of pitched battles fought by Roman soldiers. The shape of the fourth-century army grew out of long years of internal conflict.

The emperors of the early Principate took great care to maintain the loyalty of the army and were largely successful in this aim. There was nearly a century between Actium and the outbreak of widespread

Shapur I was the son and successor to the founder of the Sassanid dynasty, Ardashir I. He campaigned with great success against the Romans, defeating and killing the emperor Gordian III in 244 and capturing Dura Europus in 255. In this relief from Nagshe Rostam, another emperor, Valerian, is shown cowering in front of the king after his defeat and capture at Edessa in 260. One lurid tradition claimed that after his execution, Valerian's body was stuffed and put on display.

conflict at the suicide of Nero in AD 68, and an even longer period before the great wars following the assassination of Commodus in 193. There were attempted rebellions by provincial governors in between these massive struggles, but none gained much momentum. Some emperors met violent ends, but their deaths and the succession were usually decided in Rome. The Praetorian Guard had long played an active role in politics, notably proclaiming Claudius emperor following the murder of Caligula and auctioning the Empire to the highest bidder after the assassination of Pertinax. No emperor could survive without a loyal guard and most took care to treat the Praetorians well: they enjoyed far better conditions than the legionaries, serving for only sixteen years, receiving higher pay and frequent lavish donatives. Emperors like Galba and Pertinax, who failed to satisfy the guardsmen's expectations with suitable rewards, met swift ends. Since no emperor wished to give command of the only troops in Rome to a potential rival, the Praetorians were commanded not by senatorial officers but by equestrians. Power and the succession remained focused on Rome, but this began to change slowly as emperors such as Trajan and Hadrian spent long periods in the provinces. Marcus Aurelius fought for years against the tribes on the Danube, dying on campaign in 180. Septimius Severus, who had fought a long civil war and then led an army against the Parthians, died in 211 at York (Eboracum) where he was wintering during a campaign against the Caledonians. More than twenty emperors held power briefly until the accession of Diocletian in 284, and there were many more usurpers who failed to establish themselves and died in the process. Civil wars were common and the majority of emperors died violent deaths, frequently at the hands of their own soldiers.

As emperors spent more time with the armies in the provinces, so these began to behave in a similar way to the guard. The situation was worsened by changing patterns in the appointment of the senior officers of the army. The tradition began to change whereby Rome's armies were commanded by senators who interspersed periods of military service with civil appointments. The presence of the emperor with the army encouraged especially lavish rewards for the men who distinguished themselves in his campaigns. An increasing number of equestrian officers were elevated to the Senate and went on to hold even greater military responsibility. Marcus Aurelius promoted a prefect of an *ala*, Marcus Valerius Maximus, giving him senatorial rank and making him legate of six legions in succession, because he had killed with his own hand a king of a Germanic tribe, the Naristae. The future emperor Pertinax is said to have failed to gain a commission as a legionary centurion, but, having accepted the prefecture of an auxiliary cohort instead, served with such distinction in equestrian posts that he became a senator. Severus raised three new legions (I–III Parthica), but entrusted their command to equestrian prefects rather than senatorial legates. Through the third century the number of senior army positions held by senators gradually declined. Far more opportunities lay open to equestrians, especially those who campaigned under the emperor himself.

The equestrian officers who dominated the third-century army were in many respects professional soldiers, owing their advancement purely to their military record and the favour of the emperor. The successful men were career soldiers who served with the army continuously and did not hold civil offices. It was usually these men and not the ordinary soldiers who plotted to murder an emperor and nominated a usurper from their group. It is possible, but by no means certain, that the rapid promotion and great responsibilities given to equestrians who distinguished themselves increased the quality of the senior officers of the Roman army. The distancing of prominent senators from the command of armies may at first have been intended to prevent potential rivals from gaining support in the army. In the long term it had the effect of making usurpations more common. Long service with the army allowed this new breed of professional officers to develop strong bonds with the junior officers and soldiers. A senator hoping to gain the Imperial throne needed to be confident of at least a fair degree of support and acceptance within the Senate if he was to stand much chance of a successful reign even after he had achieved military success. In practice this reduced the number of potential rivals to a relatively small group, primarily those able to achieve command of one of the large military provinces. The emperor's frequent absence from Rome distanced him from the political world of Senate and capital, moving the court to the army. Since popularity with the soldiers and especially their officers was all that was necessary to reach the throne, it became far easier for usurpers to mount a successful challenge. Once they had attained power then this depended on the continued support of their own forces and on having greater military strength than any other rival. Several of the most successful emperors of the second half of the century came from a small group of 'Illyrian' officers, a number of whom proved very able. Internal instability had led to losses and defeats on all frontiers of the Empire and further encouraged internal rebellions. Each emperor was required to campaign with little break, since he could rarely afford to entrust the command of a major army to a potential rival. When the emperor chose to operate for any length of time in one theatre of operations there was a great danger that other parts of the Empire, feeling that their own difficulties were being neglected, would create a rival. A measure of stability was created by one of the 'Illyrian emperors', Diocletian, who gradually developed a system of dividing the imperial power, known as the Tetrarchy. This was not entirely without precedent: for instance Marcus Aurelius had ruled jointly with Lucius Verus until the latter's death. In its evolved form there were two senior emperors, each known as Augustus, who ruled the eastern and western provinces respectively, assisted by a junior colleague or Caesar. Diocletian became Augustus in the east and chose another Illyrian officer, Maximian, as his colleague in the west. The system was designed to provide enough commanders to deal with several crises simultaneously, but, by nominating the *Caesares* as successors to their senior colleagues, to prevent civil war by providing for the ambitions of all men with armies. However, the system collapsed almost as soon as Diocletian and Maximian went into voluntary retirement in 305, in the main because it failed to make provision for members of the Imperial family who were not appointed to the Tetrarchy. The principle of divided power did last for much of the fourth century, apart from the period from 324–37 when Constantine managed to achieve sole power, but usurpations and civil war continued to be common. It is frequently forgotten that Constantine, the most successful emperor of the period, spent half of his reign as a usurper. The different grades of Caesar and Augustus and the acknowledgement of the east–west division allowed ambitious generals to progress in stages to ultimate power, but also left greater potential for compromise between rivals.

The strategy in civil wars was invariably simple. Unless a compromise was reached, such as the recognition of the rival as a 'junior' Caesar or as Augustus in the other half of the Empire, then the conflict only ended with the death of one of the rivals. Both sides gathered as large an army as they could and sought out a battlefield encounter. Such a clash was only delayed as each side sought to fight the battle in the most favourable circumstances or attempted to persuade the rival army to defect. It is only in civil wars that we hear of the cautious jockeying for position before a battle which was such a feature of earlier warfare. Fighting a similarly trained and equipped enemy denied the Romans the advantages they normally enjoyed in wars against foreign opponents, and placed great emphasis on mobilizing greater numbers of troops. Civil wars drew a high proportion of the army's strength away from the defence and control of the provinces.

THE LATE ROMAN ARMY

There were several significant changes made to the structure of the Roman army during the third and fourth centuries. While the overall number of troops under arms had probably increased, the size of individual units, especially the legions, dwindled. By the end of the third century there were more than sixty legions in existence that seem to have had a theoretical strength of about a thousand men, 20 per cent of their earlier size. In 212 Caracalla had extended Roman citizenship to the greater part of the Empire's population, removing much of the distinction between citizen and non-citizen troops. The new units of cavalry titled *vexillationes* and the old *alae* and infantry cohorts seem to have mustered around five to six hundred men apiece. The equipment and training of legions and auxiliary infantry seems to have been virtually identical, fighting as close-order troops in the battle line. In the third century the rectangular *scutum* and the heavy *pilum* became less common and were replaced by oval or round shields and lighter spears such as the *lancea*. Some units also carried as many as five lead-weighted darts (*plumbatae* or *mattiobarbuli*) slotted into the hollows of their shields. Reconstructions have suggested that these had a range of about 30–65 metres (99–215 feet), more than double that of a *pilum* and significantly more than most javelins. Most units seem to have worn scale or mail armour and iron helmets if these were available. The tactics of later Roman infantry were less aggressive than those of the early Principate and in some ways more akin to those of their Polybian predecessors. Ammianus describes Roman infantry raising the *barritus*, a Germanic war cry which steadily increased in volume, in order to build up their own confidence before they entered hand-to-hand combat. The single volley of *pila* thrown just before contact was replaced by a much longer barrage of darts, javelins and frequently arrows fired by archers in close support. The charge of barbarian infantry was sometimes met at the halt, sacrificing the moral lift given in an advance to ensure that the stationary Roman line remained in good order and delivered the greatest possible number of missiles. However, faced with the numerous archers of the Persian armies, it was more common to sacrifice order and advance at a run,

This detail of the Arch of Galerius at Salonika shows a battle scene from his campaign against the Persians at the end of the third century. The Roman troops are depicted wearing scale armour and carrying round or oval shields. They carry vexilla *flags and the snake-like* draco *standards, where a multi-coloured fabric tube streamed out behind a bronze animal head, like a modern wind-sock. On Trajan's Column these standards were carried by the enemy, but we hear of their use by the Roman cavalry as early as Hadrian's reign.*

minimizing the time spent in an exchange of missiles in which the enemy would probably prove superior.

It is possible that the average unit in the later army did not have the discipline required to advance slowly and in silence, waiting until very close range before delivering a single volley of *pila* and charging into contact. The shock tactics of the early Principate were probably a more effective way of producing a decisive result in an infantry clash and winning a pitched battle. However, as we shall see, the fighting of pitched battles had ceased to be the main concern of the Roman army by the fourth century. The 5,000-strong legion had been designed for big battles, its commander controlling a sizeable section of the line and supplying units for each of the multiple supporting lines of the army's formation. The later army maintained the traditional Roman emphasis on the use of reserves, deploying into more than one line as a matter of course. The smaller size of its units meant that, while each formed an effective part of any line, they had little experience of operating in mutual support and lacked a command structure to facilitate the use of reserves. In the defeat at Adrianople one unit of Batavi placed in reserve could not be found when it was needed.

It has often been claimed that cavalry assumed a greater importance in the later army, although it has proved difficult to trace any specific changes. In part, this view derived from a misunderstanding of the great importance of the auxiliary horsemen of the Principate. Although a slight change is possible, there is no good evidence for a significant increase in the proportion of horsemen, and the ideal as in earlier periods was to have a balanced army composed of both foot and horse, the latter always in a minority. The number of heavily armoured units, *cataphractoi* and *clibanarii*, did increase, especially in the eastern army which often had to face the equally heavily armoured cavalry of the Persians. However, the vast majority of Roman cavalry continued to be trained to fight with missiles or mount a charge, and the specialist shock cavalry were not more numerous than the units of specialist light horsemen.

One of the most significant changes in the structure of the later army was the division between the troops of the field armies, the *comitatenses*, and the troops assigned to the border areas, the *limitanei*. This development occurred gradually and was not completed or perhaps officially sanctioned until Constantine. For most of the Principate the Roman army had been distributed mainly in the frontier provinces, with few troops being stationed in the interior of the Empire. Severus stationed one of his newly raised legions, Legio II Parthica, near Rome which, combined with his enlarged Praetorian Guard, provided a force of about fifteen thousand infantry and two thousand cavalry at his immediate disposal. Gallienus seems to have concentrated legionary vexillations and élite cavalry units in the approaches to northern Italy. Diocletian and Maximian gathered high-quality units into their *comitatenses*, including some élite Pannonian legions, although the size of these forces was not as great as the fourth-century field armies. Traditionally it was assumed that this trend towards troop concentrations within the Empire supplied a need for strategic reserves, allowing the emperor to cope with hostile incursions which could no longer be stopped by the troops deployed as a cordon around the frontier. This view is not supported by the evidence. Severus came to power after a long civil war, and his need for personal security was probably the main reason for the creation of an army in Italy. Gallienus had lost most of the eastern and western provinces of the Empire, hence the need for loyal troops to protect the areas which he did control. The tetrarchs similarly needed to maintain their rule by military force, although they returned the vast majority of troops to the frontiers. Constantine, victor in a civil war and insecure for at least the first half of his reign, created the large field armies. The *comitatenses* provided the emperor's ultimate guarantee of power, protecting him against political rivals. His control of such an army increased the likelihood of his support in provinces eager to be protected by concentrated forces positioned to deal with their local problems. All these forces, from Severus' Italian troops to the fully developed field

Hunting scenes like these mosaics from the Imperial Villa at Piazza Armerina in Sicily are a common feature of the art of Late Antiquity. They frequently show soldiers without armour and bareheaded, but carrying their shields. Hunting was popular with army officers from the early Empire onwards.

armies, did provide the basis for campaigning armies whenever the emperor decided to wage a foreign war or had to retrieve a major disaster somewhere in the Empire. The field armies gave the emperor personal security and the ability to wage war when required, but proved very much a two-edged sword. An emperor could not afford to leave a concentration of troops where it might be suborned by a rival. He needed to keep close control over the *comitatenses*, but this close contact with the troops made it harder to ensure their loyalty. The field armies were responsible for the murder of many emperors and the elevation of their replacements.

The *limitanei* were the troops allocated to the command of the officers (*duces limitis*) who controlled the regions into which the Empire was now divided. They were most certainly not a local militia of farmer soldiers as has often been claimed, but units of the regular Roman army. The *limitanei* carried out duties ranging from internal security, the policing of roads, defence against banditry and raiding, as well as support for officials such as tax collectors and magistrates. The commanders of the *limitanei* were powerful men in the day-to-day life of the provinces. They fulfilled all the duties which had tended to devolve on any Roman unit stationed in one locality for any length of time since the beginning of the Principate. Usually the unit occupied several posts within the region, and frequently was broken up to provide many small detachments. The *limitanei* were used to oppose small-scale enemy threats, and might also be added to a field army operating in the area; they seem to have performed well in both roles. Units detached to a field army for a long period assumed the grade of *pseudocomitatenses*.

The field armies were mobile in the sense that, unlike the *limitanei*, they were not tied to a particular frontier region which would suffer in their absence. Their removal from the frontiers and concentration, usually in or near cities, in theory meant that they were not called upon to perform everyday policing and administrative duties. Their mobility and availability as strategic reserves should not be exaggerated. The speed of a field army was never faster than that of a marching infantryman. An even greater restriction on their actions was the need to supply a force en route to and in the campaigning area. Major foreign expeditions took at least a year's preparation before they could be launched. Constantine appointed two senior subordinates, the *magister equitum* and the *magister peditum*, and under these were counts (*comites*) who might command smaller detachments. In 350 there were three major field armies, in Gaul, Illyricum and the east, but by the end of the century smaller forces had been created in Africa, Britain, Spain, on the Upper and Lower Danube and Thrace. This was in part a result of the inability of the larger field armies to deal with problems arising simultaneously in different provinces, but was also a reflection of the trend towards decentralization of authority in the late Empire.

The soldiers of the later army remained long-service professionals, although various forms of conscription became more common methods of recruitment than voluntary enlistment. Sons of soldiers were forced to serve in the army and local landlords were obliged to supply a set quota of men. Military service was not always popular and there were frequent attempts to avoid it, not least by landlords who were reluctant to see their labour force reduced. However, once in the army men seem to have adapted to a military career. Our sources make frequent mention of desertion, but this had always been a problem for the professional army and it is impossible to gauge whether or not the situation had worsened. Under the Principate the supply of recruits seems to have been adequate to maintain the professional army, which only grew slowly from the size set by Augustus. Levies often occurred

The decorated tunics worn by these men, white or off-white with darker colour circular patches and borders, were standard military dress in Late Antiquity. Poor evidence for the colour of Roman uniforms suggests that white or off-white was the most likely shade, with officers probably wearing brighter white clothing, or possibly red.

before major wars to bring existing units up to strength, but it was difficult to raise large numbers of whole units at short notice. During the Pannonian and German crises Augustus had recourse to recruiting units of freed slaves, while Marcus Aurelius employed units of former gladiators in his Danubian campaigns. The professional army simply did not possess the great reserves of manpower of the old citizen militia. The expansion of the army in the fourth century, combined with a probable decline in the Empire's population, made it even harder for later emperors to raise large numbers of troops quickly.

The units of the field armies were graded as either *palatini* or *comitatenses*, the former being the more senior. There was also a complex system of seniority between individual units, as well as units titled *seniores* and *iuniores*, presumably the result of the division of some units at an unknown date. The units of the *auxilia palatina* gained some prominence and a high reputation for effectiveness in the fourth century. Raised under Diocletian and Constantine, these units do not seem to have differed that significantly in their recruitment or training from the *auxilia* of the Principate. Some of these units and other parts of the army were recruited wholly or in part from barbarians from outside the Empire. Many recruits came from the *laeti*, groups of barbarians settled on land within the Empire, but it seems that most of these did not serve in distinct units. By the latter half of the fourth century increasing numbers of senior officers appear with 'barbarian', frequently Germanic, names. One German king, Vadomarius, ruler of the Brisiavi, an Alamannic people, was arrested by the Romans after leading raids into the Empire. He later became a *dux* in the eastern army, holding several responsible commands and fighting with some distinction for Rome. The use of such foreign troops had a long and distinguished history in the Roman army. The third century had seen the officer corps dominated by members of the aristocracy of the Danubian provinces, who either were, or became, as a result of their military service, Roman citizens and equestrians. Usually both officers and men were absorbed into the pattern of service normal to the Roman army. There is little evidence to suggest that the quality of the army was affected by the recruitment of barbarians. Officers in particular were usually employed away from their place of origin, but most of the foreign recruits seem to have been happy to fight for Rome, even against their own people. The adoption of the Germanic war cry, the *barritus*, by at least some Roman infantry may have been a result of the influx of Germanic recruits. Equally it may have been adopted by the Romans because they were aware that the Germans found it intimidating. Until large contingents of barbarians began to serve in distinct units under their own leaders there does not appear to have been any reduction in the army's fighting ability as a result of its recruitment patterns.

BARBARIANS AND THE WESTERN EMPIRE

Traditionally it has been assumed that Germanic society changed in the second and third centuries, the small individual tribes coalescing to form great tribal confederations that posed a far greater threat to the security of the Empire. When these groups came under pressure from peoples migrating from further east, the Roman Empire was unable to sustain their onslaught and collapsed. The long series of wars fought by Marcus Aurelius against the Marcomanni and Quadi is supposed to have foreshadowed the emergence of powerful peoples like the Alamanni and the Franks who were to ravage Gaul in the third century. This view is at best an exaggeration. Tribal peoples had long displayed a tendency to unite under a strong, charismatic leader, but such developments rarely outlived this man. Arminius had led a confederation of tribes against Rome until he was assassinated by rival noblemen. Prior to this he had defeated Maroboduus, king of the Marcomanni, who had created a strong power base by adding subject tribes to his own people. In neither case did a similarly strong leader appear to unite these tribes for well over a century. Most of the tribal peoples of Europe seem to have existed in a continuous cycle of

1. Romans suspicious of ambush in the broken ground. The Roman left flank commanded by Seveus halts

2. Remainder of Roman line advances and Germans advance to meet them

3. Roman cavalry and German cavalry engage heavily. Fight sways one way then the other. Roman cavalry panic whilst reforming and flee towards the second line of the Roman infantry

4. The infantry remain steady in the face of this panic. The cavalry begin to rally behind the formed infantry. The process is aided by Julian who arrives, presumably with his 200 bodyguard cavalry

5. Continued German pressure on the first Roman line. The Batavi and the Regii are sent forward to reinforce the veteran Cornuti and Bracchiati in the front ranks

unification and fragmentation. It is possible that the presence of the Roman Empire did encourage the trend towards unification. The payment of subsidies and the supply of large quantities of prestige goods allowed noblemen to build up their following and strengthen their position within the tribe. Roman attacks upon a tribe may also have encouraged support for leaders who fought successfully against

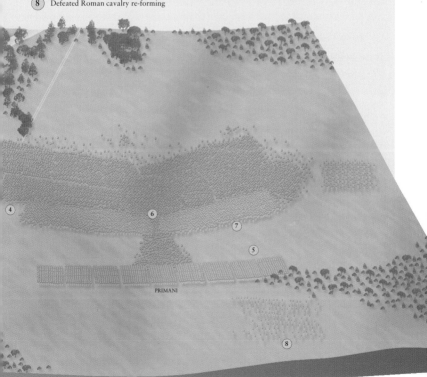

⑥ A group of Germans led by several of their kings surge forward to break the stalemate in the centre. They penetrate the Roman first line and advance against the Primani in the centre of the second line. This Legion remains firm

⑦ Gradual Roman pressure along the whole line causes the Alamanni to collapse. They suffer heavy losses in the pursuit. 243 Romans are killed

⑧ Defeated Roman cavalry re-forming

THE BATTLE OF STRASBOURG
In 357 the Caesar Julian led an army of 13,000 men against a confederation of the Alamanni, allegedly numbering 35,000 men. Its discipline and command structure gave the Roman army great advantages over the Germanic tribal forces, but even so the battle was hard fought.

PRIMANI

Rome. However, any change was one of degree and did not affect the fundamental nature of tribal society.

Most aspects of Germanic society, especially their military institutions, changed very little from the first to the fourth centuries. Even peoples such as the Alamanni, Franks and Goths were usually disunited, each geographical unit of settlements, the clan or canton, being ruled by its chief or sub-king. At some periods a single nobleman might be acknowledged as leader of several neighbouring clans. Armies continued to consist of a small permanent element, the warriors (*comites*) supported by each nobleman, and the mass of warriors composed of all free men able to equip themselves. It is difficult to estimate the scale of tribal armies with any precision. In 357 two Alamannic kings who were supported by other sub-kings and chieftains are credited with a force of thirty-five thousand men composed of their own war bands, warriors from their cantons and some mercenaries from outside the tribe. It is doubtful whether Germanic armies were ever able to muster more men than this in one place, and even this size was exceptionally uncommon. We are told that one of the two leaders of this army had two hundred warriors in his immediate following or *comitatus*, but this was probably unusually large.

The most common threat presented by the Germanic peoples was not invasion by large armies but small-scale raiding. The Romans continued to employ many of the techniques discussed in the last chapter to deal with this, joining in the patterns of intertribal warfare, but on a larger scale. Active diplomacy was combined with military action. Roman garrison commanders entertained tribal leaders to feasts and gave them gifts of money and prestige goods, emulating the methods by which powerful noblemen displayed their power in barbarian society. At formal negotiations with tribal leaders the Romans paraded their military might, the emperor receiving the envoys on a podium surrounded by the serried ranks of his splendidly equipped soldiers. Occasionally a massive attack was despatched against a people perceived to be especially hostile, settlements burnt

These scenes from the Arch of Constantine show the mixture of re-used and new material employed in its construction. In the middle is a long scene showing fourth-century soldiers attacking a walled city. They carry large oval shields and wield spears. In Late Antiquity the old taboo against showing Roman dead on monuments was abandoned and Constantine was happy to represent the enemy rout in his victory over the Roman army of his rival Maxentius at the Milvian Bridge in 312.

and the population massacred or enslaved. Sometimes columns advanced from different directions to increase the element of surprise and hinder any organized opposition. Some expeditions were prepared by feats of engineering such as the bridging of the Rhine or Danube, displaying both Rome's might and her willingness to employ massive force against her enemies. If the problems on the western frontiers seemed worse in the third and fourth centuries this was more because of Rome's internal weakness than a result of an increased barbarian threat. Raiding grew in scale and intensity when Rome's frontiers were perceived to be vulnerable due to her garrisons being drawn off to fight in interminable civil wars. Successful raids by one people encouraged other tribes to attack, a process which occurred without any need for tribal unification or widespread 'conspiracies'. Rome relied on maintaining an aura of overwhelming might and invincibility to overawe her tribal neighbours. Whenever this façade was shattered by defeats, the Romans had to fight very hard to re-establish it.

One role of the *limitanei* was to cope with small-scale raids, and their widespread distribution in vulnerable areas helped them to accomplish this task. Many Roman forts of the later Empire were very small, but they allowed the army to maintain a visible presence over a large area. A recent study by H. Elton suggests that the reason why our sources never mention raids by fewer than four hundred men was that they were usually stopped by the border troops. Larger raids took time to muster, during which the Romans hoped to hear of the threat. It was difficult to intercept a large raid as it attacked. The frontier was too long and the number of Roman troops too small to prevent these incursions; there was inevitably a delay between the Romans receiving a report of an attack and the despatch of a force of *comitatenses* to deal with it. A raid tended to become more vulnerable in proportion to its success. As the war band gathered booty its speed of movement was reduced. If the warriors chose to ravage a wide area they were forced to split up into smaller and more vulnerable parties. Mobile columns, drawn largely from the *comitatenses*, moved swiftly to intercept the raiders as they withdrew. The Romans aimed to surprise and ambush the barbarians, if possible slaughtering them with minimum loss to themselves.

Much of the fighting in the west was on a very small scale. The main difficulty for the Romans was locating the often small groups of raiders and then approaching them undetected. This required great skill from the Romans' scouting parties and a high level of initiative and ability from the Roman commanders down to the most junior levels. In 366 the scouts sent by Jovian, a *magister equitum*, located a group of Alamanni resting by a river after the sack of some villas. Jovian's troops approached, concealed from view in a wooded valley, surprised the

Germans as some were drinking and others dyeing their hair red, and destroyed them in a sudden attack. If the barbarians were well prepared or in a good position, then the Romans might hesitate before attacking them directly. Julian spent two months blockading a party of six hundred Franks who had occupied two derelict Roman forts in the winter of 357. When the Franks finally surrendered they were conscripted into the Roman army and sent to the east. It is interesting that this party is said to have decided to stay for the winter in Gaul because, since Julian was too pre-occupied fighting the Alamanni, they believed that they would be able to loot the surrounding area unmolested.

In nearly every case tribal attacks were not intended to seize territory but to gather booty and retire. Sometimes the approach of a Roman force was enough to persuade the raiders to leave without any actual fighting. During the third century most towns in the Empire acquired fortifications, something that had rarely been seen as necessary in the past. When raids were reported and the local troops unable to cope with them, the practice was for the population to retire to fortified strongholds taking moveable goods, animals and food with them. The Germans possessed little knowledge of siegecraft and were usually unable to feed themselves for the duration of a prolonged blockade. Cities were sometimes surprised and stormed by direct assault, especially if their defenders were few, or alternatively surrendered when they despaired of relief. Letting raiders retire without suffering any defeat did little to deter future attacks. Allowing raiders to range far into the provinces before they were attacked did not represent a deliberate policy of defence in depth, but an acceptance of the army's inability to prevent such incursions. Despite this acceptance, Roman operations were still dominated by the aggressive response to incursions, hunting down even the smallest bands and defeating them in detail. In this small-scale warfare the Romans enjoyed considerable advantages. Their organized system of logistics allowed them to feed and maintain a force in the field at any time of year, unlike their tribal opponents. German raiders relied on surprise and speed for success, but it is striking how often the Romans used these very qualities to defeat them. The preferred Roman tactics were those of concealment, rapid movement and ambush. High-quality, disciplined regular soldiers were more effective at this low level of warfare than the tribesmen whose cultural tradition was to fight in this way. A tribal band of even a few hundred let alone a few thousand warriors was an unwieldy body, difficult to manoeuvre with skill.

The military doctrine of the late Roman army seems to have become geared for this low-level warfare. The Romans displayed a marked reluctance to confront the German tribes in open battle if this could possibly be avoided. This is in marked contrast to the army of the early Principate which, even though it was able to adapt to lower level warfare, usually seized any opportunity to face the enemy in battle. As we have seen, the unit structure of the earlier army, especially the legion of five thousand, was well suited to pitched battle, but by the fourth century the army was structured around much smaller basic units. Blocks of five thousand men were no longer useful sub-units in field armies which were tending to become quite small. Julian led thirteen thousand men at Strasbourg, and it seems unlikely that Valens had much more than twenty thousand at Adrianople. These were both very respectable armies for the period and it is likely that most campaigning was carried out by significantly smaller forces. Relatively small transfers of four to six units between field armies seem to have had considerable significance. For most operations planned to harass Germanic raiders, small forces of a few thousand were far more suited to the task, being faster and easier to control. On those occasions when the tribes did muster a large army it might prove necessary to face them in open battle. The fourth-century army won far more battles than it lost, but the consequences of defeat were dreadful. Heavy losses to well-trained manpower were to be avoided, since such troops could rarely be replaced in the immediate future, but far more significant was the blow to Roman prestige. Rome's relations with her tribal neighbours were based upon maintaining an aura of invincibility and nothing weakened this more than a defeat in battle.

The later army lacked the ability and the confidence of the earlier army with regard to pitched battles, but it is important to place this judgement in perspective. The fourth-century army was still significantly more effective in massed battles than its tribal opponents. When large forces were sent to ravage the territory of hostile tribes the object was now to create as much devastation and terror as possible to persuade the tribes to come to terms, not to provoke them into a pitched battle in which their forces could be destroyed. The later army specialized in fighting lower scale conflict because this was the task most frequently required of it. This represented the best way of employing its high-quality manpower to defeat the enemy at minimum cost to themselves and Rome's prestige. Defeat in a small encounter did not threaten the stability of a frontier although a series of defeats might do so. It is difficult to know when this transition occurred between an army that actively sought pitched battles and one that was reluctant to fight. Our sources for the second and third centuries are so poor that any gradual change cannot be traced. It is possible that the frequent use of legionary vexillations rather than full legions suggests that much warfare was fought on a small scale even in the early Principate.

SASSANID PERSIA AND THE EAST

The Parthians had never posed a real threat to Rome's control of Syria, nor had the Romans proved able to amass the resources and undertake the massive effort of conquering Parthia. Conflicts between the two powers had tended to focus on domination of the areas between their frontiers, especially the kingdom of Armenia. Trajan's conquests in Mesopotamia had been abandoned by or soon after his death. At the end of the second century AD Severus created a permanent province of Mesopotamia, maintaining a permanent Roman presence east of the Euphrates. In 224 the last Arsacid king, Artabanus V, was defeated and deposed by a rebellion led by the Sassanid Ardashir. The Sassanid monarchy was stronger than its Parthian predecessor, but still faced the

The Roman fort at Qasr Bsheir in Jordan dates to the reign of Diocletian. Its desolate location prevented the theft of its stone for re-use in more recent buildings and ensured its remarkable preservation. Even the inscription recording its construction by the governor of Arabia in AD 292–305 remains in place over its gateway. Like most Late Roman bases it is very small, covering only 0.3 hectares and providing stabling for sixty-nine mounts, but has formidable defences. Walls are higher than in the early Empire and the corner towers now project in front of the walls, to provide enfilade fire against any attackers. The term fort is far more appropriate for these sites than the large barracks of the earlier period.

problem of controlling a disparate collection of royal lands, city states, sub-kingdoms and powerful noble families.

The Sassanid army was composed of royal troops and mercenaries, as well as feudal contingents supplied by the noblemen. Like the Parthians its main strength lay in its cavalry, the cataphracts and horse-archers. Although heavily armoured and equipped with lances for a massed charge, Sassanid cataphracts often displayed a preference for using their bows to deluge the enemy with arrows and wear him down gradually. The standard of individual training in horsemanship, archery and use of personal weapons was very high, but the level of training at unit level probably varied considerably. On several occasions the caution and good order of the Persian cavalry, especially in pursuing a beaten enemy or rallying quickly after a mounted charge, was noted by Roman sources. Persian armies tended to deploy in three distinct bodies, the centre and two wings, and often made use of reserve lines. Rarely would all three parts of the army attack simultaneously and often some sections would advance and then feign retreat to draw incautious pursuers on to the well-formed reserves. To their cavalry the Sassanids added Indian elephants carrying towers containing bowmen on their backs. Elephants intimidated the enemy by their size and frightened horses by their appearance and smell. Sometimes they created panic and disorder in the enemy ranks, making an opening which might be exploited, but they were vulnerable to missile fire, and of less use against steady troops. Numerous infantry accompanied the armies in the field, providing more archers and spearmen, but their quality was universally described as very low. Peasants impressed for service with the king, the infantry added to the spectacle created by the Persian army, but were not capable of standing up to good enemy infantry, and at best provided rallying points for the cavalry. One of the most significant differences between the Persian and Parthian armies was the far greater ability displayed by the former in siegecraft. Improved logistical organization allowed the Persians to supply a static force for the duration of a siege. Their armies also included the engineers required to construct and operate siege towers, rams and catapults, and displayed a willingness to accept the casualties inevitable in the storming of strong fortifications.

The Sassanids claimed to be the successors to the Acheamanid Persia, the empire that had been overrun in a few years by the savage onslaught of Alexander the Great. As such their propaganda laid claim to all the old realms of the Persian Empire extending up to the coast of Asia Minor. They reinstated the dominance of the old religion of Persia, Zoroastrianism, the influence of which sometimes gave their wars a strongly religious quality. The Sassanids have often been perceived as a

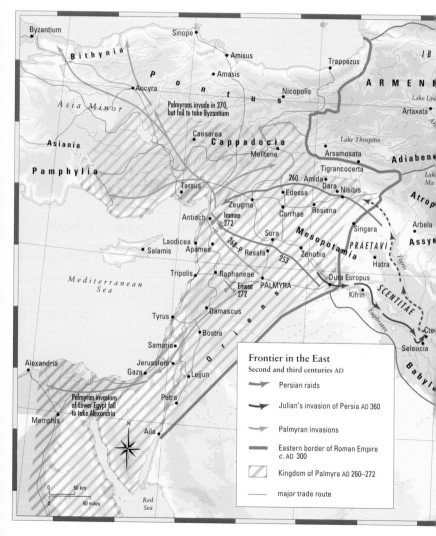

Byzantium
Sinope
Amisus
Trappezus
B i t h y n i a
P
o
n
t
u
s
Ancyra
Amasis
Nicopolis
Asia Minor
Palmyrans invade in 270, but fail to take Byzantium
ARMENI
Lake Lyc
Artaxata
Asiania
Caesarea
Cappadocia
Melitene
Lake Thospitis
Arsamosata
Adiaben
Pamphylia
Tigrancocerta
260 Amida
Dara Nisibis
Tarsus
Zeugma
Edessa
Atrop
Antioch
Immae
272
Carrhae
Resiana
Singara
Arbela
Sura
Mesopotamia
PRAETAVI
Assy
Laodicea
268-9 Resafa
Zenobia
Hatra
Salamis
Apamea
253
Tripolis
Raphaneae
Dura Europus
SCENTITAE
Mediterranean Sea
Emesa
272
PALMYRA
Kifrin
O
r
i
e
n
s
Tyrus
Damascus
Cte
Bostra
Seleucia
Samaria
Babyl
Alexandria
Jerusalem
Gaza
Lejjun
Palmyran invasions of Lower Egypt fail to take Alexandria
Petra
Memphis
Aila
N

Frontier in the East
Second and third centuries AD

→ Persian raids

→ Julian's invasion of Persia AD 360

→ Palmyran invasions

━━ Eastern border of Roman Empire c. AD 300

▨ Kingdom of Palmyra AD 260–272

── major trade route

0   50 km
0   50 miles

Red Sea

far more dangerous enemy to Rome than the Parthians had ever been. However, the Persians had as little success as the Parthians in maintaining a long-term presence west of the Euphrates in Cappadocia or Syria. The invasions which penetrated deep into the Roman East retained the character of large-scale raids. The Sassanid kings were rarely secure enough in their own realms to permit a concerted effort of conquest. Their main objective was to dominate the areas on the fringes of the two empires and in particular to drive back the Roman presence in Mesopotamia and Arabia. This could be achieved by direct attack on the Roman strongholds in this area, or by threats to Rome's provinces or military victories which allowed the Persians to gain favourable treaties with Rome.

The campaigns between Rome and Persia came to be dominated by the border fortresses, places like Nisibis, Amida and Dura Europos. Well fortified and garrisoned, they were difficult for either side to capture without large forces and considerable effort. As in the west, raiding became the most common activity for both sides. Both sides began to enlist the nomadic tribes of the area, the *Saraceni*, employing their mobility and predatory talents to raid the other's territory. Only in major expeditions were battles between the two sides at all likely, and even then the Persian objective was often to mount a display of force to allow favourable negotiations. Large royal armies with

ROME'S EASTERN FRONTIER
The long struggle between Rome and Sassanid Persia was focused around the control of the border fortresses, like Dara, Nisibis, Amida, and Dura Europus. The loss of one of these fortresses was a major disaster for either side, greatly affecting the balance of power. A more serious threat to the stability of the Roman east came during the Palmyran rebellion of AD 262–73, when Queen Zenobia's armies overran Syria and much of Egypt and Asia Minor. This was finally suppressed by Aurelian who followed up his victories at Immae and Emesa with the siege and capture of Palmyra itself.

Palmyra was a desert kingdom which flourished within the Empire from its position astride the main trade route with the Orient. Here the triad of main Palmyran deities are shown wearing lamellar armour and with swords at their belts. In the chaos produced by Shapur I's invasion, Palmyra became the leader of the eastern provinces in the effort to repel the invaders. After the death of its King Odenathus, who operated as a general of the Roman army, his widow Zenobia led a briefly successful attempt to create a new eastern empire based on Palmyra. Syria, and much of Egypt and Asia were overrun, and it was not until the emperor Aurelian defeated the Palmyrans in 272 at Antioch and Emesa that the rebellion was suppressed. Zenobia was captured and led in Aurelian's triumph, living out the remainder of her life in exile near Rome.

their full complements of elephants and infantry moved in a rather stately fashion, presenting an image of great force, but lacking the flexibility of smaller, predominantly cavalry armies.

Persian doctrine stressed that battles should only be risked when the army enjoyed great advantages of position and numbers.

Roman attacks on the Persians were more determined, and conformed to their traditional view of warfare as a life-and-death struggle. Julian amassed sixty-five thousand men for the two armies which comprised his invasion of Persia, probably the largest Roman force ever seen in the fourth century. A competently handled Roman force composed of reliable infantry and cavalry could usually defeat significantly larger Persian armies, but it proved difficult to gain much advantage from such successes. The Persians, like the Parthians before them, usually struck at the Romans' lines of communication or raided into the eastern provinces to draw the invaders off. Julian inflicted several battlefield defeats on the Persians, but his most important successes came from the capture of forts and cities. Several Roman armies in the third and fourth centuries pressed on into Babylonia, sacking Ctesiphon, the old seat of the Arsacids, and still an important centre. Yet the total defeat of Persia was a massive undertaking, requiring huge resources of manpower and logistic support and involving long years of bitter campaigning. Julian's expedition failed because he was unable to supply his vast army. As a result of this balance of power, conflict continued to consist principally of sporadic raiding from the border fortresses. Control of these allowed domination of the area and Ammianus was incensed when Julian's successor Jovian, eager to extricate himself from the failed eastern enterprise, abandoned Nisibis, Singara and territories on the border.

DISASTER AT ADRIANOPLE

In 378 the eastern emperor Valens fell, along with many of his officers and two-thirds of his army, fighting against a Gothic army at Adrianople. It was a major disaster, but its consequences should not be exaggerated. The defeat was largely the result of Valens' mistakes and not of the army's inefficiency, although it may have reflected the unpreparedness of the fourth-century army for operating in large numbers. After the battle the Romans reverted to the low-level harassing operations in which the fourth-century army excelled, and by 382 the Goths accepted peace terms and provided troops for the Roman army in subsequent years. Adrianople was a setback and a significant blow to Rome's prestige, but it was not an indication of a decline in quality of the army. At the end of the fourth century it was unlikely that anyone could have imagined that the Empire would ever cease. Certainly the tribal peoples which forced their way through the frontiers in the west did not aim to destroy Roman power, but to create a favourable place for themselves within the Roman system.

Potentially the army of the late Empire was as efficient a fighting force as any earlier Roman army. Its professionalism, discipline, training

and good equipment, supported by a well-organized logistical system, gave the Roman army significant advantages over any opponent. Well led, a Roman army was able to defeat larger enemy forces. Not all units of the army reached the highest standards of discipline and confidence in the fourth century, but this had also been true in earlier centuries. It took long years of successful campaigning to raise troops to the peak of efficiency. The fourth-century army lacked some of the flexibility in fighting different scales of warfare that had marked the army of the

Principate. It excelled in lower-level operations, but its unit and command structure was less suited to large battles. This was a reflection of the raids and skirmishing that were the most common types of combat experienced by the late Roman soldier. A reluctance to escalate a conflict and reach a swift decision by defeating the enemy in battle was a marked change from earlier practices. Roman warfare lacked something of the relentless quality that at earlier periods had distinguished it. Far more conflicts ended in treaties that did not give Rome total victory.

The synagogue at Dura Europus was richly decorated with murals showing Old Testament scenes. The figures are depicted in contemporary third-century costume, the Israelite warriors dressed as Roman soldiers. The warriors depicted wear iron scale armour, have long, hexagonal shields decorated with horizontal bars, and carry swords. Also shown are unarmoured and shieldless cavalrymen thrusting long lances underarm.

However, while the later army had the potential to be very efficient it was able to fulfil this potential less often. Its command structure was heavily divided at all levels, from the imperial power downwards. This made it difficult to co-ordinate operations on an Empire-wide basis. The *limitanei* were tied to distinct regions which suffered if they were removed and even the *comitatenses* gradually became divided into increasingly numerous regional field armies. The large number of *duces* and *comites*, and the division between civil and military administration, often made it unclear who was responsible for dealing with problems on the frontiers and slowed the process of mustering and supplying an army. Emperors found themselves having personally to direct very small-scale operations as the only way of ensuring that something happened. Frequent civil wars, the only conflicts in which battles were common, wasted the strength of the army in costly campaigns, while denuding the frontiers of troops and allowing external threats to grow. The only guarantee of power became the army, but the closer and more immediate link between soldiers and emperors only increased the chance of usurpation. The weakness of central authority encouraged the development of regional power, which could only be maintained by

the presence of troops. There were probably more soldiers under arms in the late Empire, but it was far harder to amass armies of more than twenty thousand, and dangerous to involve them in conflict for too long in any one area. Expediency, especially during civil wars, encouraged emperors to seek recruits wherever they could be found and sometimes led to unwise concessions to tribes.

The Roman Empire did not fall quickly despite all these internal weaknesses. Its own strength, derived from the successful absorption of so many peoples and the prosperity which it had brought to the provinces, was still great. Added to which, the external threats it faced were always sporadic, disunited and weak. Political divisions weakened the Roman army, but it still proved capable of winning most of the wars it was called upon to fight. Civil wars sapped Rome's military strength, but their frequency was a direct result of the failure of central authority to control the army.

Ruins of the frontier city of Dura Europus, captured by Shapur I in about 252 and never reoccupied. Traces have been discovered of the final siege, including a tunnel dug by the Persians to undermine the city wall. The Romans dug a counter-mine to attack it, but the whole thing collapsed, trapping attackers and defenders alike.

Collapse in the West, Recovery in the East

The Romans had always relied upon recently defeated enemies to provide the next generation of Roman soldiers. Barbarian tribesmen were recruited to employ their ferocity against the Empire's foes. In this frenzied scene from Trajan's Column, an auxiliary infantryman fights on, whilst holding the severed head of a previous Dacian victim by the hair between his teeth. The use of barbarian soldiers was nothing new in Late Antiquity.

Collapse in the West,
Recovery in the East

IN 418 A GROUP BASED around the Gothic tribes which had destroyed Valens' army was settled by treaty on land which was to become the Visigothic kingdom of Aquitaine. For the first time, but not the last, the western emperor acknowledged the existence of a king within the provinces, who supplied troops fighting under their own leaders and not as part of the regular army. The term *foederati* increasingly came to be used for soldiers fighting for Rome under this type of arrangement, rather than as a general term for foreign recruits in regular units. The Goths had proved too strong to destroy, but they were also a tempting source of recruits for emperors starved of readily available military manpower. They had sometimes fought against Rome, but more often on her behalf in both foreign and civil wars, although the distinction between the two was often blurred; they were also sent against the Vandals in Spain, another group of barbarians who had established themselves within the Empire. Isolated in an often alien environment, and commanded by a series of strong war leaders who operated both within and outside the hierarchy of the Roman army, the Visigoths had become more united than most tribal peoples. There is a fierce debate over whether their experiences after crossing the Danube created or merely accelerated this process.

Later in the century other peoples emulated the Visigoths in establishing kingdoms within the provinces, either by force or treaty. In 429 the Vandals took Africa, denying the western emperor access to its large revenue and rich recruiting grounds. Later, Franks and Burgundians settled in Gaul, while the Ostrogoths overran Italy. In the short term some of these groups were used to bolster an emperor's power, but in the longer term they promoted the final collapse of central authority. The western emperors were no longer able to enforce their will or guarantee protection to the provinces still loyal to them, which in turn encouraged frequent local usurpations. The infrastructure to support a large, well-trained army, and to control and supply it in the field was no longer there. Some high-quality units still existed and displayed their skill in the low-level warfare in which the later army excelled, but the number of such troops was dwindling. The army which Aetius led to blunt the onslaught of Attila's Huns at Chalons was largely composed of *foederati*. The western empire fell when central authority collapsed, and in its place emerged numerous smaller states based on a mixture of barbarian and Roman institutions, whose power and prosperity were dwarfed by comparison with the Rome of even a century before.

In the east the emperors' power remained strong. The culturally more coherent, densely populated and prosperous eastern provinces were able to maintain a large and efficient army. This preserved the balance of power on the frontier with Persia. In the sixth century the last real attempt at regaining the lost provinces in the west was made when Justinian sent armies under gifted generals such as Belisarius and Narses to destroy the Vandals in Africa and the Ostrogothic kingdom in Italy. Although the campaigns were successful, in the long term it proved impossible for the Romans to retain control of the old provinces around the Mediterranean. The Empire's resources were sufficient for its defence, but utterly inadequate for overseas conquest.

The army of the sixth century represented the culmination of many of the trends already observed in the army of late antiquity. Many soldiers were under arms and included on the Imperial army's strength, but forces in the field were seldom large. Belisarius landed in Africa with only sixteen thousand men, and his first expeditionary force to Italy numbered half that total. Armies of twenty-five thousand or more were exceptionally rare. A late sixth-century military manual, *Maurice's Strategikon*, discussed armies of five to fifteen thousand men, but clearly viewed forces towards the lower end of this scale as the norm, and believed twenty thousand men to be an unusually large force. The basic unit consisted of two to five hundred men led by a

The Roman Empire in AD 418

The Roman Empire in AD *418 was divided into many small provinces and regions. Many of the army units listed for each command may have existed only in theory or been mere skeletons.*

WESTERN DIVISION

Britanniae
1. Valentia
2. Britannia II
3. Flavia Caesariensis
4. Britannia
5. Maxima Caesariensis

Galliae
1. Ludgunensis III
2. Ludgunensis II
3. Belgica II
4. Germania II
5. Ludgunensis Senonia
6. Ludgunensis I
7. Belgica I
8. Germania I
9. Maxima Sequanorum

Septum Provinciae
1. Aquitanica II
2. Aquitanica I
3. Novem Populi
4. Narbonensis I
5. Viennensis
6. Narbonensis II
7. Alpes Maritimae

Hispaniae
1. Gallaecia
2. Carthaginiensis
3. Tarraconensis
4. Lusitania
5. Baetica
6. Insulae Balearum
7. Tingitania

Africa
1. Mauretania Caesariensis
2. Mauretania Sitifensis
3. Numidia
4. Africa
5. Byzacena
6. Tripolitania

Italia
1. Alpes Cottiae
2. Aemilia
3. Raetia I
4. Raetia II
5. Liguria
6. Venetia et Histria
7. Flaminia et Picenum

Suburbicaria
1. Corsica
2. Sardinia
3. Tuscia et Umbria
4. Valeria
5. Picenum Suburbicarium
6. Roma
7. Campania
8. Samnium
9. Bruttii et Lucania
10. Apulia et Calabria
11. Sicilia

Pannonia (to ca.400); Illyricum (after ca. 400)
1. Noricum Ripense
2. Noricum Mediterraneum
3. Pannonia I
4. Valeria
5. Savia
6. Pannonia II
7. Dalmatia

EASTERN DIVISION

Dacia
1. Moesia I
2. Dacia Ripensis
3. Praevalitana
4. Dardania
5. Dacia Mediterranea

Macedonia
1. Epirus Nova
2. Macedonia
3. Epirus Vetus
4. Thessalia
5. Achaea
6. Creta

Thraciae
1. Moesia II
2. Scythia
3. Thracia
4. Haemimontus
5. Rhodope
6. Europa

Asiana
1. Hellespontus
2. Phrygia Pacatiana
3. Phrygia Salutaris
4. Asia
5. Lydia
6. Pisidia
7. Lycaonia
8. Caria
9. Pamphylia
10. Insulae
11. Lycia

Pontica
1. Bithynia
2. Honorias
3. Paphlagonia
4. Helenopontus
5. Pontus Polemoniacus
6. Galatia
7. Armenia I
8. Galatia Salutaris
9. Cappadocia II
10. Cappadocia I
11. Armenia II

Oriens
1. Isauria
2. Cilicia I
3. Cilicia II
4. Euphratensis
5. Mesopotamia
6. Syria
7. Osrhoene
8. Cyprus
9. Syria Salutaris
10. Phoenice
11. Phoenice Libanensis
12. Palaestina II
13. Arabia
14. Palestina I
15. Palestina Salutaris

Aegyptus
1. Libya Superior
2. Libya Inferior
3. Aegyptus
4. Augustamnica
5. Arcadia
6. Thebais

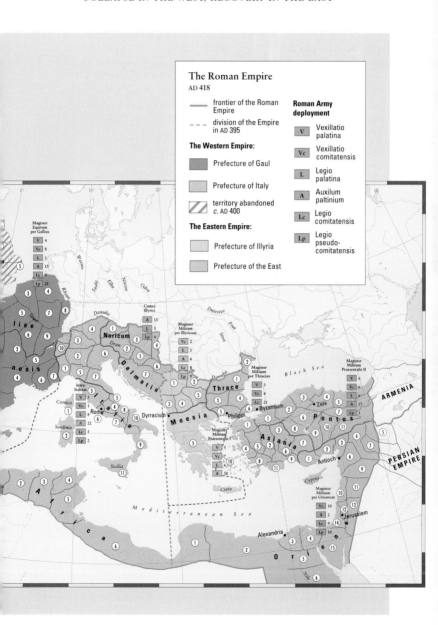

The Roman Empire
AD 418

⎯⎯⎯ frontier of the Roman Empire

- - - - division of the Empire in AD 395

The Western Empire:

Prefecture of Gaul

Prefecture of Italy

territory abandoned c. AD 400

The Eastern Empire:

Prefecture of Illyria

Prefecture of the East

Roman Army deployment

V	Vexillatio palatina
Vc	Vexillatio comitatensis
L	Legio palatina
A	Auxilium paltinium
Lc	Legio comitatensis
Lp	Legio pseudo-comitatensis

The great aqueduct supplying the Roman colony at Caesarea on the coast of Judaea. Originally built by Herod the Great, the aqueduct was restored and substantially widened by a vexillation of Legio X Fretensis during the reign of Trajan. The inscription recording this work is still in situ on one of the arches. Some of the finest engineers in the Empire were numbered amongst the ranks of the legions, and they were often called in to undertake or supervise building projects. However, in the late Empire, the resources and willingness to undertake such major works were less common. Running parallel with the Roman aqueduct is the line of the subterranean Byzantine aqueduct. This was a reasonably effective way of supplying water to the city, but far less visually spectacular.

tribune, several of these combining to form a *moira*, commanded by a *dux* in battle. The larger armies often proved difficult for their commanders to control before and during a battle, and several defeats were blamed on undisciplined troops who had forced their general to risk battle unnecessarily. In a pitched battle the traditional Roman emphasis on using reserves still dominated military doctrine, although it was rare for the whole army to be divided into several lines of roughly equal size and composition. The late fourth-century theorist Vegetius had recommended avoidance of battle unless the circumstances were very favourable indeed, but the author of the *Strategikon* was even more cautious and advocated it only as a last resort. Theory was reflected in practice, with the conflicts of this period tending to be long, but including very few massed actions. Campaigns in both east and west were dominated by raids, skirmishes and sieges. In the wars with Persia the border fortresses continued to play a dominant role as bases from which mobile columns set out to plunder enemy territory. It is unlikely that either side ever thought in terms of total victory, realizing that they no longer possessed the necessary resources. The Persians' main objective was often to exact a sizeable payment from the Romans in return for peace, money which helped the Sassanid monarch to maintain his position and defend against attacks by the Huns from the Caucasus to the north. The control of the border fortresses remained of central importance and the Roman decision to build a new stronghold at Dara, directly opposite Persian controlled Nisibis, was viewed as a provocative act.

The division between the *limitanei* and *comitatenses* remained, although some of the latter became permanently garrisoned in frontier strongholds and may have differed little from the border troops. Units of *foederati* in the eastern army were little different from the ordinary *comitatenses*, being paid and fed by the state and serving under Roman appointed officers. The main distinction was that they included a higher proportion of barbarian recruits. The best element of field armies was often provided by the *bucellarii* who, although they took an oath of loyalty to the emperor, were effectively the household troops of the senior commanders. A successful leader such as Belisarius amassed several thousand of these soldiers and trained them to a high level of efficiency. The *bucellarii* also included a pool of officers who might be employed to command army units. In addition there were allied contingents, most commonly Arabs or Saraceni in the wars with Persia. These fought both with the field armies and independently when hired to raid the emperor's enemies.

The strength of the sixth-century army was undoubtedly its cavalry. The majority were equipped equally for shock action or for fighting from a distance. These horsemen wielded lance or bow as the situation demanded, but although the riders were heavily armoured, their horses do not seem to have been protected. The *Strategikon* emphasized the need for cavalry to charge in a disciplined manner, always maintain a reserve of fresh troops, and be careful not to be drawn into a rash pursuit. *Bucellarii* were normally cavalry, and by their nature horsemen were more suited than foot soldiers to the raids and ambushes which dominated the warfare of this period. The sixth-century cavalryman was far more likely to experience combat than his infantry counterpart. In a large-scale action a well-balanced mix of horse and foot was still the ideal, but the Roman infantry of this period had a very poor reputation. In part this was a result of their inexperience, but they often seem to have lacked discipline and training. Narses used dismounted cavalrymen to provide a reliable centre to his infantry line at Taginae. At Dara Belisarius protected his foot behind specially prepared ditches. Roman infantry almost invariably fought in a defensive role, providing a solid base for the cavalry to rally behind. They did not advance to contact enemy foot, but relied on a barrage of missiles, javelins, and especially arrows, to win the combat. All units now included an element of archers and it was claimed that Roman bows shot more powerfully than their Persian counterparts. The front ranks of a formation wore armour and carried large round shields and long spears, but some of the ranks to the rear carried bows. Infantry

This fragment of a frieze now in the Louvre probably dates to the reign of Marcus Aurelius and shows Roman soldiers attacking a barbarian village. Punitive expeditions in which houses were burnt, cattle confiscated and slaves taken were standard practice for the Roman army of most periods.

formations might be as deep as sixteen ranks. Such deep formations made it difficult for soldiers to flee, but also reduced their practical contribution to the fighting, and were another indication of the unreliability of the Roman foot soldier. The *Strategikon* recorded drill commands given in Latin to an army that almost exclusively spoke Greek. There were other survivals of the traditional Roman military system, many of which would endure until the tenth century, but the aggressive, sword-armed legionary was now a distant memory.

THE END OF THE EMPIRE

The collapse of central authority in the west had encouraged the trend towards increasingly small-scale warfare. Local warlords and landowners, who based their power on the number of armed retainers they controlled, flourished. One of the reasons why archaeologists have found so few traces of the devastation supposedly wrought by barbarian invaders is that most of these moved in relatively small bands whose depredations affected only a small area. The fragmentation of political power ensured that there were seldom enough soldiers stationed in one area or concentrated in field forces free to range throughout the provinces to oppose successfully all the groups of invaders, or overawe the tribes that had been settled inside the Empire.

The basic pattern that warfare would assume for the next thousand years, at least in Europe, had already been set in the late Roman period. Medieval warfare was characterized by raids and skirmishes, frequently revolving around the possession of fortified strongholds. The pitched battle was a relatively rare occurrence, and the idea of the decisive battle had lost the central place which it had occupied in earlier antiquity. Vegetius, the fourth-century military theorist who had been one of the first Roman authors to advocate the avoidance of battle, remained highly popular throughout the Middle Ages. The Byzantine army endured and preserved many of the traditions of the professional Roman army but in the west no kingdom possessed the strong central authority or the wealth to support a large permanent army of uniformed, drilled and disciplined soldiers.

There had been a close relationship between the army and political life from very early on in Rome's history, when political rights were granted to those able to equip themselves to fight in the main battle line. Under the Principate, when the emperors had taken care to ensure that the army was personally loyal, its senior commanders had still been drawn from the ranks of Rome's aristocracy. In the third century this connection had been broken and the army's generals were career soldiers serving permanently with the army and owing their progress entirely to Imperial favour. Gradually the hatred and fear which the prosperous, literate classes had always felt towards the professional soldier was extended to his officers. The army now made and maintained an emperor in his position, and the wishes of even the wealthiest sections of the rest of society counted for little. There was little to check the regionalism of troops stationed for long periods in one area, and often recruited there as well, since the generals were no longer serving for a short tour, nor drawn from a central pool without regional ties. Civil war after civil war sapped the Empire's strength and further encouraged the growth of local powers who could offer protection to a region.

Morale obviously has had massive significance throughout military history, but this was especially true when battles were decided by massed, hand-to-hand fighting. One defeat often prompted another since troops who had lost their confidence could rarely stand up to the pressures of close combat no matter how superior their training, organization or tactics were to those of the enemy. The difficulty of restoring soldiers' belief in the possibility of success after a series of defeats was demonstrated by conflicts as separated in time as the Numantine war and the early sixth-century campaigns with Persia. It was not just this tactical dimension which suffered from a series of defeats. At a strategic level the Romans relied on the domination of their neighbours, securing the Empire's frontiers through overawing the peoples outside by creating an impression of overwhelming might. Defeats seriously weakened this façade of Roman strength and meant that the Romans had to fight very hard to recreate it. From the middle of the third century onwards the Romans were never able to restore the situation fully, a trend which was marked by the abandonment of the relentless pursuit of total victory that had been the traditional hallmark of Roman military practice. The insecurity of the later emperors made this attitude impractical.

The western empire did not fall, nor did the east endure because of the results of a few decisive battles. The external threats to Rome were unconcerted and sporadic, and not enough in themselves to have destroyed the Empire. The professional Roman army was capable of defeating any of the opponents faced in Late Antiquity as long as it was given the resources of men and material to do so. The failure of the Roman state to control the professional army, and in particular its officer corps, steadily destroyed the central power that controlled the infrastructure necessary for the army to function. The institutions of the Roman army gradually disappeared in a process lasting centuries, but the idea of the professional army would later have a great impact on the rise of modern warfare in the Europe of the sixteenth and seventeenth centuries.

Conclusion

The Roman army changed the world, creating an Empire the legacy of which is still felt today. Much of Europe employs a legal system based on Roman law and speaks languages derived from, or heavily influenced by, Latin. The dominance of the West in the last few centuries extended both languages and legal systems throughout most of the globe. Until the last few generations Greek and Latin languages and literature lay at the heart of western education and cultural life.

The idea of the Roman army and the power of the Roman Empire long epitomised splendour and majesty. Napoleon gave his regiments eagles as their standards, included *velites* in his Guard and dressed his heavy cavalry in classically inspired helmets. The armies of Russia and Prussia both bore eagles on their flags, and the names of their rulers, Tsar and Kaiser, were

Hadrian's Wall remains one of the most visually impressive monuments left by the Roman army, although only in places is it visible on the ground. This is Milecastle 39, west of Housesteads fort in the central section running along some of the most spectacular scenery.

derived from Caesar. Even the nascent United States chose the eagle for its standard and drew on Roman models for its political institutions.

Physical remains of the Roman army are dotted throughout Europe, North Africa and the Near East. It is impossible to stand on the siege ramp at Masada and not marvel at the skill and determination of the men who built such a thing in that appalling landscape, simply to prove that no fortress was impregnable to them. At the other end of the Empire, the remains of Hadrian's Wall impress in a different way, from their sense of scale, solidity and permanence. Many of the finds from these sites are very human – gaming dice, remains of meals such as oyster shells, the superbly preserved shoes from Vindolanda, and, famously, the communal latrine at Housesteads. The inscriptions found in the forts and settlements of the area reveal a very cosmopolitan community, soldier and civilian mixed, worshipping gods from all over the known world. Yet however many races were recruited into the ranks of the army they were at least partially absorbed into its uniform culture. In the garrisons at Masada and Vindolanda two unknown Roman soldiers idly scrawled a line from Virgil's epic the *Aeneid* on a piece of papyrus and a wooden writing tablet respectively.

Several factors explain the Roman army's long success: discipline, training, good equipment and well-organized logistic support were all important factors, but other armies had these without achieving as much. The Roman military system was characterized by its flexibility. The same basic structure could adapt to local conditions and defeat very different opponents. In time the Romans became as adept at raids and ambushes as any irregular tribesmen, yet preserved their superiority in massed battle. The Romans always fought aggressively, whether in open battle or on a smaller scale, ever assuming the offensive and trying to dominate the enemy. This, combined with their refusal to admit defeat and their willingness to accept heavy losses, made the Roman army extremely difficult to beat. Yet, ultimately, much depended on the Romans' ability to absorb others, to turn the enemies of today into the Roman soldiers of tomorrow.

Appendices

APPENDIX A: THE CAREER PATTERN (CURSUS HONORUM) OF ROMAN SENATORS IN THE SECOND CENTURY BC *(Chapter 3)*

Min. Age	Magistracy	Number	Responsibilities
			Ten years military service in cavalry or on the staff of a relative/family friend needed to qualify for political office. In practice this rule may not have been rigidly enforced.
30	Quaestor	8–12	Financial administration at Rome and in the provinces; acted as second in command to governors.
36	Aedile	4	No military responsibility, but administrative role at Rome; an optional post.
39	Praetor	6	Judicial function at Rome; commanded provinces not allocated to consuls; usually controlled one legion + allies, but occasionally larger forces.
42	Consul	2	Most senior executive officers of state; governed larger provinces and given command in all major wars; usually controlled two legions + two allied *alae*.
–	Censor	2 every 5 years	No actual military command, but most prestigious magistracy reserved for most distinguished ex-consuls.

All magistracies apart from the censorship were held for a single year. All members of a magisterial college held equal power. The numbers of quaestors and praetors gradually increased as further provinces were added to the empire. However, until the very end of the Republic there were only ever two consuls per year.

Appendix B: The Legion of the Early Principate *(Chapter 4)*

OC – *Legatus Legionis* (Senatorial officer serving for *c.* three years).

2ic – *Tribunus Laticlavius* (Senatorial officer serving for *c.* three years).

3ic – *Praefectus Castrorum* (Experienced officer, usually former *primus pilus*).

Staff including: five *Tribuni Angusticlavii* (equestrian officers serving for *c.* three years, who have already commanded an auxiliary cohort and may go on to command an *ala*).

First Cohort – 800 men in five centuries of 160 each, commanded by five centurions ranked in order of seniority:
primus pilus; princeps; princeps posterior; hastatus; hastatus posterior

Nine other cohorts – 480 men in six centuries of a centurion, *optio, signifer,* and *tesserarius*, plus eighty men. The centurions ranked in order of seniority:
pilus prior; pilus posterior; princeps prior; princeps posterior; hastatus prior; hastatus posterior

The ranks of the cohorts included many specialists and HQ personnel who spent much of their time on detached duty. Other units included:

The Cavalry – 120 men whose internal organization and command structure is unclear.

The Veterans – men who had served twenty years. They may have formed a separate unit or formed part of the first cohort.

Artillery – Vegetius claims that each cohort operated a large stone-throwing engine, whilst each century crewed a light bolt-shooter. The amount of artillery employed by a legion probably varied according to the situation.

APPENDIX C: SIZE AND STRUCTURE OF AUXILIARY UNITS – FIRST TO EARLY THIRD CENTURY AD *(Chapter 4)*

Unit title	Infantry (centuries)	Cavalry (turmae)
Cohors Quingenaria Peditata	480 (6)	None
Cohors Quingenaria Equitata	480 (6)	120 (4)
Cohors Milliaria Peditata	800 (10)	None
Cohors Milliaria Equitata	800 (10)	240 (8)
Ala Quingenaria	None	512 (16)
Ala Milliaria	None	768 (24)

Quingenary units were normally commanded by a prefect. Milliary units and units of Roman citizens were commanded by tribunes.

APPENDIX D: ACTUAL STRENGTH RETURNS FOR THREE QUINGENARY MIXED COHORTS SHOWING VARIATION FROM THEORETICAL STRENGTH *(Chapter 4)*

Date	Unit	Infantry	Horse	Total 1	Total 2
c. 100	Cohors I Hispanorum Veterana	417	119	536	546
156	Cohors I Augusta Lusitanorum	363	114	477	505
213–16	Cohors I Apanenorum	334	100	434	457

Total 1 is without officers or supernumeraries. Total 2 includes officers and in the case of the second two cohorts small detachments of camel-riders (dromedarii) employed for patrolling in desert regions. The totals of all three cohorts included a significant number of officers and men absent on detached duties.

APPENDIX E: STRENGTH RETURN OF COHORS I TUNGRORUM
C. AD 92–7 *(Chapter 4)*

This table shows the wide dispersal of and range of duties performed by a
Roman garrison (Tab. Vind. II. 154).

18 May, total number of First Cohort of Tungrians, commanded by the
Prefect Julius Verecundus, = 752, including 6 centurions. From these are
absent:

guards of the governor (*singulares legati*) – 46
at the office of Ferox (possibly a legionary legate) – unreadable
at Coria (Corbridge) – 337 including 2 centurions
at London – 1 centurion
unreadable – 6 including 1 centurion
unreadable – 9 including 1 centurion
unreadable – 11
at ?unreadable – 1
unreadable – 45
Total absentees – 456 including 5 centurions

The remainder, present with the unit – 296 including 1 centurion – from these:
sick – 15
wounded – 6
suffering from eye inflammation – 10
sub-total – 31
remainder, fit for duty – 265 including 1 centurion

*Although milliary, the cohort appears to have had only six centuries. The high
proportion of men, and especially five out of six centurions, can only have made it
difficult for the cohort to train and drill as a unit.*

Glossary

Dates in brackets give an approximate indication of period.

ala: (1) Term used under the Republic for the contingents of Italian allies, roughly equivalent in size to a Roman legion. The name meant 'wing' and derived from the standard formation of a consular army that placed two legions in the centre with an *ala* on either flank (late fourth to second century BC). (2) Term used for the cavalry units of the Imperial *auxilia*. These were either 512 or 768 strong and commanded by a prefect or tribune respectively (first to third century AD).

aquilifer: The standard-bearer who carried the legion's standard (*aquila*), a silver, later gold, statuette of an eagle (first century BC to third century AD).

auctoritas: The informal reputation or prestige of a Roman politician which determined his influence in the Senate and was greatly added to by his military achievements (third to first century BC).

auxilia: Troops recruited from non-citizens, the *auxilia* of the Principate provided a valuable source of extra manpower for the Roman army, as well as the vast majority of its cavalry. They were not organized into legion-sized units, but into cohorts and *alae* (first to third century AD).

ballista: A two-armed, torsion catapult capable of firing bolts or stones with considerable accuracy. These were built in various sizes and most often used in sieges (third century BC to sixth century AD).

beneficiarius: A grade of junior officer usually recruited from experienced rankers who performed a range of policing and administrative roles often detached from their units (first to third century AD).

bucellarii: The household troops paid and supported by particular commanders, although nominally loyal to the emperor. The *bucellarii* were usually high-quality cavalry. The name derives from *bucellatum*, the army's hard-tack biscuit, and emphasized the commander's obligation to feed and provide for his men (fourth to sixth century AD).

cantabrian ride: A drill practised by the Roman cavalry during which men rode in turn towards a target, wheeling to the right at short range and then riding parallel, keeping their shields towards the target. The object was to maintain a continual barrage of missiles at a single point in the enemy line, weakening an enemy before launching a charge sword in hand. Similar tactics were employed by cavalry, especially horse-archers, of many nations (first to sixth century AD).

cataphract: Close order, heavily armoured cavalrymen whose main tactic was the shock charge. Often the horses were also protected by armour. Their normal weapon was the two-handed lance, the *contus*, but some cataphracts carried bows as well. These troops were more common in the eastern empire.

centurion: Important grade of officers in the Roman army for most of its history, centurions originally commanded a century of 60–80 men. Under the Principate many served for very long periods and provided an element of permanence in the otherwise short-term officer corps of the legion. The most senior centurion of a legion was the *primus pilus*, a post of enormous status held only for a single year (first century BC to third century AD).

century (*centuria*): The basic sub-unit of the Roman army, the century was commanded by a centurion and usually consisted of sixty, later eighty, men (late fourth century BC to third century AD).

cheiroballista: A version of the scorpion mounted on a mule-drawn cart to increase mobility (first century BC to sixth century AD).

clibanarius (*clibanarii*): A heavily armoured cavalryman, it is unclear whether or not these were identical to cataphracts, but it is possible that the term was applied to the heaviest troops. The name derived from a nickname meaning 'bread-oven'.

cohort (*cohors*): Originally the name given to the contingents which formed the Allied *Alae* under the Republic, the cohort became the basic tactical unit of the army by the end of the second century BC. It usually consisted of 480 men in six centuries, but there were also larger units of 800 in five or ten centuries (second century BC to third century AD).

comes: Officers of the later Roman army, ranking below the *magistri militum* (late third to sixth century AD).

comitatenses: Units included in the regional forces not tied to specific frontier provinces (fourth to sixth century AD).

consul: The year's two consuls were the senior elected magistrates of the Roman Republic, and held command in important campaigns. Sometimes the Senate extended their power after their year of office, in which case they were known as proconsuls.

contubernium (*contubernia*): Term applied to the groups of eight men who shared a tent and messed together (third century BC to third century AD).

contus (or *kontos*): The long, two-handed thrusting spear employed by Parthian, Persian, Sarmatian, and later Roman cataphracts (first century BC to sixth century AD).

cornicularius: A grade of clerks included on the administrative staff of several officers in the legion (first to third century AD).

cuneus: (1) Term used for a formation intended to break through an enemy line by concentrating the moral and physical shock of a charge at a single point. It may have been triangular in shape or alternatively a deep, narrow-fronted column. (2) Term used for cavalry units of unknown size (third to fourth century AD).

decurion: Cavalry officer who originally commanded ten men. Under the Principate a decurion led a *turma* of about thirty horsemen (first to third century AD).

dictator: In times of extreme crisis a dictator was appointed for a six-month period during which he exercised supreme civil and military power. Later victors in civil wars, such as Sulla and Julius Caesar, used the title as a basis for more permanent power (fifth to first century BC).

dux: Officers of the later Roman army (late third to sixth century AD).

dux (*duces*) *limitis*: Commanders of all troops (*limitanei*) within one of the regions into which the frontier provinces of the later empire was divided (late third to sixth century AD).

equites singulares: The term used for the bodyguard cavalry attached to the staff of provincial governors under the Principate. These units seem to have been about 500 strong and were recruited from men seconded from the auxiliary *alae* (first to third century AD).

equites singulares augusti: The emperor's own horse guards for the first three centuries of the Principate, these provided an élite cavalry force to support the Praetorian Guard. They were recruited from the pick of the troopers in the provincial *alae*, and enjoyed very favourable service conditions and good chances of promotion (first to third century AD).

foederati: Allied barbarians obliged to provide military service to the emperor. They usually served in their own units and sometimes under their own commanders who usually held Roman rank. As time went on these became increasingly indistinguishable from units of the regular army, especially in the East (fourth to sixth century AD).

gladius: A sword, *gladius* is conventionally used to describe the *gladius hispaniensis*, the short Spanish sword which was the standard Roman sidearm until well into the third century AD. The weapon could be used for cutting, but was primarily intended for thrusting (third century BC to third century AD).

hasta: A spear. It has proved difficult to associate the *hasta* or the *lancea* firmly with a particular size or shape of weapon discovered in the archaeological record (fifth century BC to sixth century AD).

hastatus (*hastati*). The first line of heavy infantry in the Republican legion, recruited from younger men (late fourth to second century BC).

Hippaka Gymnasia: The cavalry games which displayed the training of the *alae* of the Principate. Intended as a spectacle the troopers were dressed in bright colours and wore highly decorated armour (first to third century AD).

imaginifer: The standard-bearer who carried the *imago* (*imagines*), a standard with a bust of the emperor (first to third century AD).

immunes: Soldiers exempt from ordinary fatigues, usually as a result of possessing special skills (first to third century AD).

imperium: The power of military command held by magistrates and pro-magistrates during their term of office (third century BC to third century AD).

laeti: Term applied to groups of barbarians settled by the emperor on land in the provinces under the obligation of providing recruits for the army. These rarely served in distinct contingents of their own (fourth to sixth century AD).

legatus (*legati*): A subordinate officer who held delegated *imperium* rather than exercising power in his own right. *Legati* were chosen by a magistrate rather than elected (third to first century BC). (1) *Legatus augusti pro praetore*: This title was given to the governors of the military provinces under the Principate, who commanded as representatives of the emperor (first to third century AD). (2) *Legatus legionis*: The title given to legionary commanders under the Principate (first to third century AD).

legion (*legio*): Originally a term meaning levy, the legions became the main unit of the Roman army for much of its history. Under the Republic and Principate they were large, predominantly infantry, formations of around four to five thousand men, but by late antiquity most seem to have dwindled to a strength of about one thousand.

limitanei: The grade of troops commanded by the *duces limitis*, the military commanders of the various regions, usually on the frontier, into which the provinces of the later empire were divided (fourth to sixth century AD).

lorica: A corselet or breastplate. The three most common types of armour were (1) *Lorica hamata* or ring-mail armour was probably copied from the Gauls. It offered good protection and was relatively simple, if time consuming, to manufacture. Its main disadvantage was its great weight, which primarily rested on the shoulders, although the military belt helped to transfer some of this burden to the hips (third century BC to sixth century AD). (2) *Lorica squamata* or scale armour was less flexible and offered poorer protection than mail. It seems to have been popular for most of the army's history, perhaps in part because it could be polished into a high sheen and made the wearer look impressive (third century BC to sixth century AD). (3) *Lorica segmentata* is the name invented by modern scholars to describe the banded armour so often associated with the Romans. It offered good protection and its design helped to spread its weight more evenly than mail, but was complex to manufacture and prone to damage, which may explain its eventual abandonment (first to third century AD).

magister equitum: (1) Second-in-command to the Republican dictator, the Master of Horse traditionally commanded the cavalry, since the dictator was forbidden to ride a horse (fifth to first century BC). (2) Title given to senior officers of the later Imperial army, equal in status to *magistri peditum* (fourth to sixth century AD).

magister militum: Title given to the senior officers of the later Imperial army (fourth to sixth century AD).

magister peditum: Title given to senior officers of the later Imperial army (fourth to sixth century AD).

maniple (*manipulus*): The basic tactical unit of the Republican legion, the maniple consisted of two centuries. It was commanded by the centurion of the right hand (senior) century if he was present (late fourth to second century BC).

mattiobarbuli: Heavy, lead-weighted darts, often carried clipped into the hollow of a shield. Also known as *plumbatae* (third to sixth century AD).

military tribune (*tribunus militum*): Six military tribunes were elected or appointed to each Republican legion, one pair of these men holding command at any one time. Under the Principate each legion had one senior, senatorial tribune (*tribunus laticlavius* who wore a wide purple sash) and five equestrians (*tribunii angusticlavii* who wore a narrow purple sash), (first to third century AD). Military auxiliary cohorts and *alae*, or those with special status, were commanded by equestrian officers called tribunes who performed an identical role to auxiliary prefects. Some regiments of the later army were also commanded by tribunes.

numerus: A vague term meaning simply unit or band, *numerus* was the title given to many units of irregulars from a common ethnic background employed for frontier patrolling from the second century AD onwards. It was also applied to some units of cavalry in the later army.

onager: A one-armed torsion catapult designed to lob stones. It was simpler in construction than the two armed *ballistae*, but heavier, less mobile, and not as accurate. The basic design was to be followed by the Medieval mangonel (third to sixth century AD).

optio (*optiones*): Second-in-command of a century, the rank was symbolized by the carrying of the *hastile*, a shaft tipped with an ornamental knob (first to third century AD).

ovatio: A lesser form of the triumph, in an ovation the general rode through the city on horseback rather than in a chariot (fifth century BC to first century AD).

palatini: Units of higher status and prestige than the *comitatenses*, the *palatini* also formed part of the field armies of late antiquity (fourth to sixth century AD).

pilum: The heavy javelin which was the standard equipment of the Roman legionary for much of Rome's history (third century BC to third century AD).

plumbatae: see *mattiobarbuli*.

praefectus castrorum: Third in command of a legion during the Principate, he was an experienced officer who was usually a former *primus pilus* (first to third century AD).

Praepositus: Unit commander of the later army, equivalent to a tribune (third to sixth century AD).

praetor: Praetors were annually elected magistrates who governed the less important provinces and fought Rome's smaller wars.

Praetorian Guard: The military bodyguard of the emperors of the Principate, the Praetorians received higher pay and donatives and enjoyed far better service conditions than the legions. For most of their history they were formed into cohorts commanded by tribunes and the whole corps commanded by two Praetorian Prefects. No emperor could afford to alienate his guardsmen who represented the main military force in Rome or Italy. They were disbanded by Constantine in 312 after supporting his rival Maxentius (first to third century AD).

prefect (*praefectus*): Equestrian commander of an auxiliary cohort or *ala* (first to third century AD).

princeps (*principes*): The second line of heavy infantry in the Republican legion, recruited from men in the prime of life (late fourth to second century BC).

principales: The three subordinate officers of the century, the *optio*, *signifer* and *tesserarius* (first to third century AD).

pseudocomitatenses. The grade given to units of *limitanei* who had become attached to the field armies (fourth to sixth century AD).

quaestor: Magistrates whose duties were primarily financial, quaestors acted as deputies to consular governors and often held subordinate military commands.

quincunx: The chequerboard formation used by the Republican legion in which the three lines were deployed with wide intervals between the maniples, the gaps being covered by the maniples of the next line. There has been much debate over the precise nature of this system, but it is clear that it gave the Roman legions far greater flexibility than the Hellenistic *phalanx* (late fourth to second century BC).

schola: The units of guard cavalry of the later Roman army. The *scholae* provided many senior commanders from among their number (third to sixth century AD).

scorpion: The light bolt-shooting *ballista* employed by the Roman army both in the field and in sieges. They possessed a long range, as well as great accuracy and the ability to penetrate any form of armour (first century BC to sixth century AD).

scutum: A shield, particularly the heavy, legionary shield. This was semi-cylindrical and usually either oval or rectangular. It was held by a single, transverse handgrip behind the central boss, although additional straps were used to support its weight on the march (third century BC to third century AD).

signifer: The standard-bearer who carried the standard (*signum*) of the century. Under the Principate they administered the men's pay and savings accounts (first to third century AD).

Socii: The Italian allies of the Republic, the *socii* formed *alae* which were normally equal in number or more numerous than the Roman troops in an army. After the Social War (90–88 BC) and the general extension of citizenship to most of the Italian peninsula the *socii* disappeared and all Italians were recruited into the legions (late fourth to second century BC).

spatha: The long sword used by the cavalry of the Principate and eventually adopted by most of the later army. It was well balanced for both cutting and thrusting (first to sixth century AD).

spolia opima: The highest honour which a triumphing general could claim was the right to dedicate *spolia opima* in the Temple of Jupiter Optimus Maximus on the Capitol. The right could only be gained by killing the enemy general in single combat and was celebrated on just a handful of occasions.

tesserarius: Third-in-command of a century, the *tesserarius* traditionally was responsible for commanding the sentries. The name derived from the *tessera*, the tablet on which the night's password was distributed through the camp (first to third century AD).

testudo: The famous tortoise formation in which Roman legionaries overlapped their long shields to provide protection to the front, sides and overhead. It was most commonly used to approach enemy fortifications and allow the legionaries to undermine them (third century BC to third century AD).

triarius (*triarii*): The third and senior line of heavy infantry in the Republican legion, recruited from veteran soldiers (late fourth to second century BC).

triumph: The great celebration granted by the Senate to a successful general took the form of a procession along the Sacra Via, the ceremonial main road of Rome, displaying the spoils and captives of his victory and culminated in the ritual execution of the captured enemy leader. The commander rode in a chariot, dressed like the statues of Jupiter, a slave holding a laurel wreath of Victory over his head. The slave was supposed to whisper to the general, reminding him that he was mortal. Under the Principate only members of the Imperial family received triumphs, but other commanders were granted the insignia of a triumph (*ornamenta triumphalia*) (fifth century BC to fourth century AD).

turma (*turmae*): The basic sub-unit of the Roman cavalry for much of its history, a *turma* consisted of around thirty men. Under the Principate it was commanded by a decurion (late fourth century BC to third century AD).

Urban cohorts: The paramilitary police force established by Augustus in Rome and a few other key cities, for instance guarding the Imperial mint at Lyon. They were organized into cohorts commanded by tribunes under the overall direction of the Urban Prefect (first to third century AD).

veles (*velites*): The light infantry of the Republican legion, recruited from the poor or those too young to fight as heavy infantry. It is unclear whether they were identical to or superseded the *rorarii*, another term applied to light infantrymen in the Republican legion (late fourth to second century BC).

vexillation (*vexillatio*): (1) A detachment operating independently, a vexillation might consist of anything from a few men to several thousand and could be drawn from several units. The use of these temporary formations designed for a specific role or operation gave the Roman army considerable flexibility (first to third century AD). (2) Many cavalry units of the later Field Armies were known as vexillations. They appear to have been similar in size to the old *alae* (fourth to sixth century AD).

vexillum: A square flag mounted crosswise on a pole, the *vexillum* was used to mark a general's position and was also the standard carried by a detachment of troops (first to third century AD).

vigiles: The paramilitary fire-brigade established by Augustus in Rome, the *vigiles* were organized into cohorts, but not equipped with weapons (first to third century AD).

Biographies
and Primary Sources

GENERAL BIOGRAPHIES

AUGUSTUS (GAIUS JULIUS CAESAR OCTAVIANUS) (63 BC–AD 14)

Caesar's nephew and adopted son, he became Rome's first emperor following the defeat of his last rival, Mark Antony, at Actium in 31 BC. During his reign he presided over the last intensive period of Roman expansion. Not an able soldier himself, he had the knack of appointing capable subordinates, notably his friend, Agrippa, and later younger family members.

BELISARIUS (AD 505–565)

An Eastern Roman general of considerable ability, especially gifted in the use of cavalry, Belisarius achieved notable successes on the Persian frontier and in Africa and Italy. His success earned him the enmity of the Emperor Justinian.

GAIUS JULIUS CAESAR (c. 100–44 BC)

Probably Rome's most successful general, he conquered Gaul (58–50), twice bridging the Rhine and leading expeditions to Britain. The decision of his former ally, Pompey, to side with his political enemies, led to the Civil War (49–5 BC), during which he won victories at Pharsalus, Thapsus and Munda. Appointing himself life dictator, Caesar was murdered by a conspiracy led by Brutus and Cassius.

CONSTANTINE I (AD 285–337)

The first Christian Emperor, Constantine spent nearly half his reign as a usurper, before establishing himself as sole ruler. His greatest military successes occurred in civil wars, notably the defeat of Maxentius at the Milvian Bridge in 312.

GNAEUS DOMITIUS CORBULO (D. AD 67)

One of the most famous Roman commanders of the *c.* 1st AD, who famously remarked on the lack of freedom of Imperial Governors to wage war compared to their Republican counterparts. A strict disciplinarian, he fought in Germany and Armenia. His reputation was such that Nero ordered him to commit suicide as a potential rival.

MARCUS LICINIUS CRASSUS (115–53 BC)

A skilled politician, Crassus was also an able commander, who systematically destroyed the slave armies led by Spartacus (71 BC). Later he led the invasion of Parthia, but a series of mistakes led to his defeat and death at Carrhae (53 BC).

GAIUS AURELIUS VALERIUS DIOCLETIANUS (AD 245–313)

Diocletian was the creator of the Tetrarchic system, dividing the empire into an eastern and western half, each ruled by an Augustus and his deputy or Caesar. Much of his career was spent in fighting domestic rivals, but he also fought a successful Persian War.

QUINTUS FABIUS MAXIMUS 'CUNCTATOR' (*c.* 275–203 BC)

Fabius was renowned as the man who saved Rome by delaying, avoiding direct confrontation with Hannibal's victorious army. Elected dictator at the age of 58 in 217, he held the consulship three times during the Second Punic War and exercised a great influence on Roman strategy for over a decade.

HANNIBAL BARCA (*c.* 247–188 BC)

Hannibal was the personification of the ideal Hellenistic general. Throughout his campaign he dazzled his opponents at the strategic and tactical levels, repeatedly achieving the apparently impossible. A leader of genius, he was able to inspire his own senior officers as much as the various races who fought in the ranks of his army. His ultimate defeat in the war with Rome has more to do with the Romans' relentless determination than his own failings.

GAIUS MARIUS (C. 157–87 BC)

Traditionally believed to be the man who converted the citizen militia into a professional army, he was a strict disciplinarian and an able commander. However, his career was unorthodox and after victories over Jugurtha and the migrating Cimbri, Marius was one of the leaders in Rome's first Civil War.

NARSES (AD 478–573)

An imperial eunuch who was given military command late in life, Narses achieved several successes in Italy when he first supported and then replaced Belisarius, winning victories at Taginae in 552 and Casilinium in 553. He made more effective use of infantry than Belisarius, using them to support his cavalry.

GNAEUS POMPEIUS MAGNUS (106–48 BC)

Pompey's career was extremely unorthodox, commanding armies in Sicily, Africa and Spain under Sulla, whilst still a private citizen. He completed the defeat of Mithridates (66–63 BC), but political failures led to his alliance with Crassus and Caesar (the first triumvirate). After Crassus' death, this broke down and led to the Civil War in which Pompey was defeated at Pharsalus (48 BC) and later murdered in Egypt.

PUBLIUS CORNELIUS SCIPIO 'AFRICANUS' (236–c. 184 BC)

The greatest Roman commander of the Second Punic War, he evicted the Carthaginians from Spain and finally defeated Hannibal at Zama. After the war he fought in Gaul and under his brother's command against Antiochus. An inspirational leader, his well-trained legions allowed him to experiment with variations on traditional Roman tactics.

PUBLIUS CORNELIUS SCIPIO AEMILIANUS (185–129 BC)

A skilled commander, Scipio was the adopted grandson of Africanus. After distinguished service in Spain and the first years of the Third Punic War, he was given the command in Africa and presided over the destruction of Carthage in 146 BC. In 133 BC he captured the Celtiberian stronghold of Numantia.

LUCIUS SEPTIMIUS SEVERUS (AD 145–211)

The eventual victor of the Civil War that followed Commodus' murder, Severus spent much of his reign on campaign. He led a highly successful expedition against Parthia and established a new province in Mesopotamia. He died in Eboracum (York) in northern Britain, having spent the last three years fighting the Caledonian tribes.

PUBLIUS CORNELIUS SULLA (138–78 BC)

Initially an associate of Marius, Sulla turned against him when the latter tried to rob him of the command against Mithridates of Pontus, and became the first Roman general to march on Rome (88 BC). After defeating the Pontic invasion of Greece (86–4 BC), Sulla returned and defeated his Roman rivals with great bloodshed (83–2 BC). Appointing himself dictator, he later retired to a life of debauchery and died soon afterwards.

MARCUS ULPIUS TRAJANUS (AD 52–117)

Adopted by the aged emperor Nerva, Trajan ascended to the throne in AD 98. During his campaigns he conquered Dacia after two fierce wars (AD 101–2, 105–6). He died during his massive Parthian expedition (113–7) and many of his eastern gains were abandoned by his successor, Hadrian.

TITUS FLAVIUS VESPASIANUS (AD 9–79)

Vespasian commanded Legio II Augusta during the invasion of Britain and was later sent to suppress the rebellion in Judaea. In the Civil War that began after Nero's death, he gained support of all the Eastern armies and eventually defeated all his rivals, later proving to be one of the better emperors.

Primary Sources

CHAPTER 1

Diodorus Siculus (*c*. 30s BC) wrote a universal history in Greek, part of which covering the period 486–302 has survived and includes some details of Roman history.

Dionysius of Halicarnassus (late first century BC) was a Greek scholar working in Rome who produced a *History of Rome*, which survives for the period to 443 BC.

Livy (59 BC–AD 17) produced a Latin history of Rome *From the Foundation of the City* (*ab urbe condita*) in 142 books, most of which have been lost. The first ten books cover the period up to 293 BC. Fiercely patriotic, Livy's military descriptions can be unreliable.

Plutarch (*c*. AD 46–120) was a Greek Biographer who produced a series of *Parallel Lives* pairing notable Greek and Roman figures. He is only ever as good as these sources, many of which no longer survive. For this period we have *Lives* of *Romulus, Coriolanus*, and *Camillus*.

CHAPTER 2

Appian (*c*. AD 95–*c*. 170) was an Alexandrian Greek writing in Rome under Antoninus Pius. Books survive from his *Roman History* covering the Punic, Macedonian and Syrian Wars.

Livy – Books 20–30 cover the Second Punic War, whilst 31–45 deal with the years up to 167 BC.

Plutarch – *Lives* of *Pyrrhus, Fabius Maximus, Marcellus, Flamininus*, and *Aemilius Paullus*.

Polybius (*c*. 203–*c*. 120 BC) served against the Romans in the Third Macedonian War after which he went as hostage to Rome where he became a close associate of Scipio Aemilianus. Originally covering 264–146 BC, he is the best source for Roman warfare in this period, but unfortunately much of his work has been lost.

CHAPTER 3

Appian provides detailed accounts of the campaigns in Spain and the Mithridatic Wars. The four books of *The Civil Wars* provide the only continuous account of the series of conflicts which caused the fall of the Republic.

Caesar (*c*. 100–44 BC) wrote *Commentaries* which, with the additional books written by some of his officers, cover the operations in Gaul (58–51 BC) and the Civil War (49–45 BC). Skilfully written pieces of propaganda, these remain an invaluable portrait of Rome's army on campaign.

Cicero (106–43 BC) was a famous orator, statesman, and prolific author, but saw very little military service. His posthumously published *Letters to Atticus* and *Letters to his Friends* include accounts of his minor campaign in Cilicia in 51–50. *Letters to his Friends* 10. 30 contains Sulpicius Galba's eye-witness account of the Battle of Forum Gallorum in 43.

Plutarch – *Lives* of *Marius, Sulla, Sertorius, Pompey, Crassus, Caesar, Antony, Brutus,* and *Lucullus.*

Sallust (86–34 BC) served under Caesar in Gaul, but was later forced from public life following a scandal during his governorship of Africa and turned to writing history. His *Jugurthine War* and *Catilinarian Conspiracy* survive along with fragments of his *Roman History.*

CHAPTER 4

Arrian (born *c*. AD 90) was governor of Cappadocia under Hadrian and produced two brief works in Greek dealing with the army's training and tactics, the *Tactica* concerning cavalry training and the *Battle Order against the Alans* describing operations in Cappadocia.

Dio Cassius (*c.* AD 163–*c.* 235) was a Roman senator from the Greek East who produced a *Roman History* which ran up to his own times. Large sections of the work, including all of the late first and second centuries AD, survive only in later epitomes.

Frontinus (AD 40–103) governed Britain in AD 74–78 and later produced a book of *Strategems* describing ploys used by commanders of the past to gain victory.

Josephus (born *c.* AD 37) was a Jewish general who fought against Rome in AD 66–7, before surrendering and changing sides. His *Jewish War* provides by far the most detailed account of the first century army on campaign. However, he tends to exaggerate his own deeds and those of his patron, the Emperor Titus.

Pseudo-Hyginus (second century AD) is the name conventionally given to the unknown author of *On the laying-out of camps*.

Suetonius (born *c.* AD 69) was a palace official at Rome who wrote biographies of Rome's rulers from Caesar to Domitian.

Tacitus (born *c.* AD 56) was a Roman senator who wrote a biography of his father-in-law, *Agricola* (who campaigned in Britain from AD 77 to 84), and an ethnographic work, the *Germania*, describing the tribes of Germany, with some mention of their military practices. Substantial fragments of *The Histories* and *The Annals* give much detail of the period AD 14–70. Tacitus was more interested in politics than war, but does provide good accounts of many conflicts.

Vegetius (late fourth/very early fifth century AD) produced an *Epitome of Military Science*, arguing for revival of traditional military drill and training. It contains many interesting comments about the earlier army, but it is often difficult to know which period he is referring to and whether he reflects the theory or actual practice.

CHAPTER 5

Ammianus Marcellinus (*c.* AD 330–*c.* 395) was a Roman officer from the Greek East who served in the army in the middle of the fourth century. The surviving books of his Latin History deal with the years 353–378. Ammianus' narrative provides us with a highly detailed picture of the later Roman army in operation.

Herodian (died *c.* AD 250) was a senator who produced a history of the Roman emperors from AD 180–238. Although often unreliable or vague, Herodian is our fullest source for this period.

The *Historia Augusta* (probably late fourth century) is a collection of biographies of most of the emperors from Hadrian to Carinus and Numerian, almost certainly the work of a single author. Its reliability is highly questionable.

The *Notitia Dignitatum* (*c.* AD 395) is an illustrated manuscript listing the officers of the later army, the units they commanded, and their stations. A valuable source, it presents many problems of interpretation.

CHAPTER 6

Maurice's Strategikon (trans G. T. Dennis (Philadelphia, 1988)) is a sixth-century military manual describing in detail the formation and tactics to be employed by Byzantine armies.

Procopius (mid sixth century) was a civil servant who served on the staff of Belisarius for several campaigns. He wrote *The Wars*, an account of the campaigns of Justinian's reign to 550/1, including conflicts with the Persians, Vandals and Goths, and the *Secret History*.

Further Reading

GENERAL

The literature on the Roman army is truly vast, much of it tucked away in academic journals inaccessible to the general reader. The works listed here will allow the interested reader to begin a deeper study into the subject.

Good general works are L. Keppie, *The Making of the Roman Army* (London, 1984) on the Republican army and G. Webster, *The Roman Imperial Army* (London, 1985: repr. with updated bibliography Oklahoma, 1998) for the Empire. Also useful are H. Parker, *The Roman Legions* (Oxford, 1928), Y. Le Bohec, *The Imperial Roman Army* (New York, 1994), and J. Peddie, *The Roman War Machine* (Gloucester, 1994), although not all of the latter's conclusions are widely accepted. A little dated and rather too dogmatic, H. Delbrück, (trans J. Renfroe), *History of the Art of War within the Framework of Political History*, vols 1–2 (Westport, 1975) still contains much of interest. Well illustrated, more general works include General Sir John Hackett (ed.), *Warfare in the Ancient World* (London, 1989), and J. Warry, *Warfare in the Classical World* (London, 1980).

A. Goldsworthy, *The Roman Army at War, 100 BC–AD 200* (Oxford, 1996) contains a detailed analysis on operational practices and the nature of battle in the Late Republic and Early empire. H. Elton, *Warfare in Roman Europe, AD 350–425* (Oxford, 1996) is an excellent and wide ranging study of the Later Roman Army. More specific studies include J. Roth, *The Logistics of the Roman Imperial Army at War (264 BC–AD 235)* (Leiden, 1999), and N. Austin and B. Rankov, *Exploratio: Military and Political Intelligence in the Roman World from the Second Punic War to the Battle of Adrianople* (London, 1995).

Military equipment is covered only briefly in this work, but there are a number of excellent books on the subject, notably M. Bishop and J. Coulston, *Roman Military Equipment* (London, 1993), P. Connolly, *Greece and Rome at War* (London, 1981), and H. Russell Robinson, *The Armour of Imperial Rome* (London, 1975). Recent research in this field is regularly published in the *Journal of Roman Military Equipment Studies*.

CHAPTER 1

A good recent survey of Rome's early history is T. Cornell, *The Beginnings of Rome. Italy and Rome from the Bronze Age to the Punic Wars (c. 1000–264 BC)*, (London, 1995). There are few books dedicated to the military history of this period, but notable articles include E. Rawson, 'The Literary Sources for the Pre-Marian Roman Army', *Papers of the British School at Rome 39* (1971), 13–31, and L. Rawlings, 'Condottieri and Clansmen: Early Italian Warfare and the State.', in K. Hopwood, *Organized Crime in the Ancient World* (Swansea, 1999).

CHAPTER 2

There are many works on this period and in particular the Punic Wars, of which the best are J. Lazenby, *The First Punic War* (London, 1996) and *Hannibal's War* (Warminster, 1978). Several interesting articles are included in T. Cornell, B. Rankov and P. Sabin, *The Second Punic War: A Reappraisal* (ICS London, 1996). Also notable are F. Adcock, *The Roman Art of War under the Republic* (Cambridge Mass., 1940), W. Rogers, *Greek and Roman Naval Warfare* (Annapolis, 1937), J. Thiel, *Studies on the History of Roman Sea-Power in Republican Times* (Amsterdam, 1946), and B. Bar-Kochva, *The Seleucid Army. Organization and Tactics in the Great Campaigns* (Cambridge, 1976).

CHAPTER 3

Important contributions on Roman imperialism are to be found in E. Badian, *Roman Imperialism in the Late Republic* (Oxford, 1968), S. Dyson, *The Creation of the Roman Frontier* (Princeton, 1985), W. Harris, *War and Imperialism in Republican Rome 327–70 BC* (Oxford, 1976), M. Hopkins, *Conquerors and Slaves* (Cambridge, 1978), and J. Rich and G. Shipley (ed.), *War and Society in the Roman World* (London, 1993). Also of great interest are P. Brunt, *Italian Manpower, 225 BC–AD 14* (Oxford, 1971), J. Fuller, *Julius Caesar: Man Soldier and Tyrant* (London, 1965), E. Gabba, *Republican Rome, the Army and the Allies* (Oxford, 1976), N. Rosenstein, *Imperatores Victi. Military Defeat and Aristocratic Competition in the Middle and Late Republic* (Berkeley, 1990), and F. Smith, *Service in the Post-Marian Roman Army* (Manchester, 1958).

CHAPTER 4

G. Cheesman, *The Auxilia of the Roman Imperial Army* (Oxford, 1914), K. Dixon and P. Southern, *The Roman Cavalry* (London, 1992), and A. Johnson, *Roman Forts* (London, 1983) all cover aspects of the army in this period. J. Campbell, *The Emperor and the Roman Army* (Oxford, 1984) is good on the political role of the army. Daily life is dealt with in R. Alston, *Soldier and Society in Roman Egypt* (London, 1995), R. Davies, *Service in the Roman Army* (Edinburgh, 1989), and G. Watson, *The Roman Soldier* (London, 1969). J. Mann, *Legionary Recruitment and Veteran Settlement during the Principate* (London, 1983) remains a fine study of recruitment.

The Empire's frontiers and the vexed question of Grand Strategy are covered by E. Luttwak, *The Grand Strategy of the Roman Empire* (New York, 1976), A. Ferrill, *Roman Imperial Grand Strategy* (New York, 1991), and B. Isaac, *The Limits of Empire. The Roman Army in the East* (Oxford, 1992). D. Kennedy and D. Riley, *Rome's Desert Frontier from the Air* (London, 1990) offers spectacular pictures of many Roman outposts, whilst a good introduction to the copious literature on Hadrian's Wall is D. Breeze and B. Dobson, *Hadrian's Wall* (London, 1987).

CHAPTER 5

A. H. M. Jones, *The Later Roman Empire* (Oxford, 1964) still contains a wealth of information concerning Late Antiquity. P. Southern and K. Dixon, *The Late Roman Army* (London, 1996) is a handy introduction, but not always reliable, whilst A. Ferrill, *The Fall of the Roman Empire: The Military Explanation* (London, 1986) offers one interpretation of the military problems of Late Antiquity. T. Coello, *Unit Sizes in the Late Roman Army.* BAR S645 (Oxford, 1996) presents the meagre evidence for unit size, as does W. Treadgold, *Byzantium and its Army, 281–1081* (Stansford, 1995).

On Roman foreign policy see D. Braund, *Rome and the Friendly King* (London, 1984), T. Burns, *Barbarians within the Gates of Rome: A Study of Roman Military Policy and the Barbarians, CA. 375–425 AD* (Indiana, 1994), P. Heather, *Goths and Romans, 332–489* (Oxford, 1991), M. Dodgeon and S. Lieu, *The Roman Eastern Frontier and the Persian Wars, 226–363* (London, 1991), and A. Lee, *Information and Frontiers* (Cambridge, 1993).

CHAPTER 6

R. Blockley, *East Roman Foreign Policy* (Leeds, 1992) is useful. C. Fauber, *Narses: Hammer of the Goths* (Gloucester, 1990) is an accessible account of this commander's career. G. Greatrex, *Rome and Persia at War, 502–532* (Leeds, 1998) is a first rate study of a single war, also containing much of more general interest.

Index